A Random Walk
to
Nowhere

How the Professors Caused a
Real "Fraud-on-the-Market"

A Random Walk
to
Nowhere
How the Professors Caused a
Real "Fraud-on-the-Market"

Edward E. Williams
John A. Dobelman

Rice University, USA

World Scientific

W JERSEY · LONDON · SINGAPORE · BEIJING · SHANGHAI · HONG KONG · TAIPEI · CHENNAI · TOKYO

Published by

World Scientific Publishing Co. Pte. Ltd.

5 Toh Tuck Link, Singapore 596224

USA office: 27 Warren Street, Suite 401-402, Hackensack, NJ 07601

UK office: 57 Shelton Street, Covent Garden, London WC2H 9HE

Library of Congress Cataloging-in-Publication Data

Names: Williams, Edward E, author. | Dobelman, John A, author.
Title: A random walk to nowhere : how the professors caused a real
    "fraud-on-the-market" / Edward E Williams, John A Dobelman,
    Rice University USA.
Description: Singapore ; Hackensack, NJ : World Scientific Publishing, [2020] |
    Includes bibliographical references and index.
Identifiers: LCCN 2019042755 | ISBN 9789811207785 (hardcover) |
    ISBN 9789811208355 (paperback)
Subjects: LCSH: Efficient market theory--Statistical methods. | Efficient
    market theory--Mathematical models. | Random walks (Mathematics)
Classification: LCC HG4915 .W55 2020 | DDC 332.01/5195--dc23
LC record available at https://lccn.loc.gov/2019042755

British Library Cataloguing-in-Publication Data
A catalogue record for this book is available from the British Library.

Copyright © 2020 by World Scientific Publishing Co. Pte. Ltd.

For any available supplementary material, please visit
https://www.worldscientific.com/worldscibooks/10.1142/11484#t=suppl

Desk Editor: Shreya Gopi

Typeset by Stallion Press
Email: enquiries@stallionpress.com

Printed in Singapore

This book is dedicated to the everlasting
memory of

M. C. Findlay, III, Ph.D.
1944–2008

and

Edward E. Williams, Ph.D.
1945–2018

Contents

Preface

This book is about an intellectual fraud. The fraud started out as an honest attempt to improve our insights on how financial markets work, but it eventually became almost a religion that every financial economist had to buy into or risk professional crucifixion. More importantly, the fraud has become a part of the legal opinion that has greatly influenced decisions all the way up to the United States Supreme Court. These decisions have real consequences and it is almost a certainty that the judges and justices who have relied on this "fraud" have no idea that their opinions have little basis in economic fact. The fraud we are describing goes by the name "the efficient market hypothesis" (or EMH). The origins of the EMH began over 50 years ago and it came to dominate research in the academic financial community for decades. In addition to the courts, the hypothesis has been widely read and considered by professional portfolio managers and every day investors. It has even been claimed to be the intellectual foundation of the development of the index fund, perhaps the greatest institutional development in finance since the creation of stock markets.

The Nobel Prize in Economics has been awarded to many of those who did the original EMH research, suggesting that the hypothesis was scientifically formulated, subject to rigorous analysis and demonstrated correct. The truth is that the EMH was always a hypothesis. It was accepted as "true" by academic financial economists, eager to prove it so because of their devotion to classical economic theory. In some respects, it was the financial version of the intellectual war between the Keynesians and the neoclassicists that has gone on since the 1930s. Indeed, the EMH debate more or less was a major battle in the "War between the Economists" that could be as figuratively bloody as any real war.

Those who believe in "free markets" are naturally attracted to the EMH because it extols the virtues of a perfectly operating market. Although more recent revisions of the EMH have eliminated the "perfection" part of the claims (due mainly to conflicts with reality), the notion that all available information is readily and correctly impounded into stock prices is still a very appealing concept to many stock market observers and participants. This has become especially so as MBAs educated at all the best places have had the theory of the EMH drilled into them for decades.

The EMH remains a dilemma for political conservatives. To a degree, it is supportive of Adam Smith's "invisible hand," the great unseen limb extension that supports most notions of capitalism. However, the idea that financial analysts come to work every day without expectations of earning "monopoly profits" by discovering information (or having unique insights) does not square with reality. The neoclassical economist says all monopolies do not last in the long-run (unless controlled by the power of the state) since the fact that someone is earning "economic rent" (profits beyond what one would expect on a risk adjusted basis) simply draws in competitors. Barriers to entry eventually fall as capital is raised to finance the competitors who have spotted the monopoly business.

This observation sounds quite reasonable to many, and in the goods and services markets (think "high tech" businesses) it might well be true. However, the financial markets are different. If every stock is considered an "information monopoly," the underlying business of each stock cannot be so forever. The question becomes one of when competition destroys the monopoly, and this is not at all easily determined. At the core of the issue is the subject of "valuation" and how much people will pay for a future income stream that might be very "uncertain." The resolution of uncertainty takes time, and those who can figure out the time path can make a lot of money.

The EMH advocates might argue the time path is "what it is" and no one can know what directions the path will take. Hence, an "efficient" market is one where no one can have particular insights over the valuation of many stocks for a long period of time and that is why "indexing" makes sense. It is very cost efficient (no "rents" paid to high-priced portfolio managers). Of course this begs the question of how stocks in the index are in markets where at least somebody or an organization has to do the work to ferret out the information that gives efficient value to the underlying stocks in the index in the first place. This discussion will occupy many of the pages to follow.

In this book, the authors have decided to use the first person to tell the story. Author Edward E. Williams observes, "When I did my doctoral work 50 years ago, the phenomenon to be discussed was in its infancy. Many of today's Nobel Prize winners were still untenured and fighting the old dinosaurs who then dominated the finance departments at major universities such as Chicago and Penn's Wharton School of Finance and Commerce (its name back then). The textbooks and even the scholarly literature were almost all verbal and institutional in content. Business schools were considered intellectual back-waters and were shocked by the findings of the two studies (one by the Ford and the other by the Carnegie Foundations). These two studies of business higher education became known by the names of their authors as the Gordon & Howell Report and the Pierson Report. These reports noted the lack of rigor in the courses taught by business schools and the poor quality of research done at these institutions. The time was ripe for economists to add the 'rigor' of their discipline to the weak offerings of the business schools."

What was an untenured professor to do? Well, for those versed in economics, the best idea was to differentiate one's product. That is, try to create a personal (or at least "personal-for-a-few") monopoly. The opportunity arose due to all the fuss about business schools being so backward. Suppose, by the introduction of mathematics into business research, the whole subject could be made "scientific." This would kill two birds with one stone. The old fogeys couldn't read your papers, and the research looked awfully imposing to deans and practitioners who hadn't a clue as to the real content of the new efforts. Author Edward E. Williams and his colleague M. Chapman Findlay, who would eventually become Chairman of the Finance Department at the University of Southern California and go on to be one of the top forensic experts in finance in the United States, played that game for a while as well until they published a damning paper in the academic practitioner journal *Financial Management* in 1980, when the EMH was still in its adolescence. This article caused quite a stir and is discussed at the beginning of Chapter 1.

In the pages to follow, we shall outline the major issues that gave rise to the fraud. But first, it might be wise to review the practical damage done by the EMH advocates. On June 23, 2014, the U.S. Supreme Court ruled in *Halliburton v. Erica P. John Fund* that investors who had been "harmed" by corporate securities fraud would be able to continue to pursue lawsuits on a class action basis and upheld the legal doctrine of committing a "fraud-on-the-market" in such lawsuits. This decision was predicated on an earlier decision in a 1988 case (*Basic Inc. v. Levinson*) which presumed that securities markets were efficient (albeit slightly qualified by the Court). Thus, the plaintiff's bar has been able to have a venue to litigate under the veil that markets are "efficient" with the result being many more class action lawsuits. In all likelihood, many of these suits are or will be settled or adjudicated to the detriment of numerous publicly held companies and their shareholders.

To an extent, our attention will focus on the role of statistics in the rise of what has been branded as "financial economics." Every attempt will be made to keep any math simple so that readers who have never heard of a mean or a standard deviation can understand what is going on. Obviously, some knowledge of elementary statistics would be useful here but this is not the place to demonstrate how to calculate basic statistics. The concepts are not difficult to understand, however.

Since the pages that follow are intended for the general public (or at least educated business and financial executives) to read and understand, some of the jargon and even concepts are explained at a level and to a degree that academics would scoff at. That is fine since this book is not for them. We have also tried to minimize any "sour grapes" to settle old scores with journal editors who for decades rejected any papers that did not follow the EMH party line. It will become clear, however, that many billions of dollars were foolishly spent on developing a complex theoretical structure which, at its basic, is only true by assumption. It will also be obvious that the numerous Nobel Prizes awarded to those who developed or laid the foundation for the EMH were hardly justified. We are certainly not alone in the view that economics in general is by no means a science (a point discussed at length later in this book), and awarding a prize for "economic science" confuses the general public into thinking the discipline is a rigorous science like physics or chemistry, which it most definitely is not.

Finally, we have provided an extensive bibliography at the end of the book for those who would like to check the facts or actually read the materials referenced in this endeavor. The text citation is to the author(s), journal (for articles), book title and year. For example, the first reference in Chapter 1, is to Frank Knight's *Risk, Uncertainty, and Profit*. The publication date is indicated as 1921. The reader may find the specifics on this book under "Knight, F." in Bibliography. The date distinguishes this reference from other articles or books by the same author. In the case of two or more pieces by the same author in the same year, the notation would be given by an "a", "b", etc. such as 1921a, 1921b, and so forth.

We recall with deepest regret the passing of Professor Williams, blessed be his memory, who departed this earth just prior to the publication of this book. Our editors Yubing Zhai and Shreya Gopi at World Scientific provided continued support, encouragement, vision, and courage for this project. The authors also thank and acknowledge Mr. David Warren and Ms. Tania C. Pinon Venegas who helped in the preparation of this manuscript.

About the Authors

Dr. Edward E. Williams was Professor Emeritus at Rice University where he taught for 36 years (1978–2014). He received his B.S.E. from the Wharton School at the University of Pennsylvania in 1966 and his Ph.D. from the University of Texas at Austin in 1968. Over the years, he has written 13 books and numerous articles and scholarly papers. He was one of the original critics of the Efficient Market Hypothesis (EMH) when it first appeared five decades ago. At Rice, he began its entrepreneurship program which is now rated as one of the top such endeavors in the world. During his teaching career, he received many awards for teaching excellence and was named by *BusinessWeek* as the "penultimate entrepreneurship professor" in the United States. He has also been Professor of Statistics at Rice where he has published numerous works in financial economics and investments. Professor Williams passed away unexpectedly on October 3, 2018.

Dr. John A. Dobelman is Professor in the Practice in Statistics, and Director of the Professional Master's Program at Rice University, Houston, Texas, USA; he has taught at Rice since 2004. Prior to that he was an Adjunct Professor in Houston's University of St. Thomas Cameron School of Business, a Pricing Scientist at PROS Holdings, Inc., and held various engineering and management positions in aviation facilities engineering and construction. His current research interests include investments analysis, stochastic modeling for markets and finance, simulation-based and quantitative portfolio selection and management, deception in patterns of noise, optimal display of quantitative information, improved communication, and applications of statistics to engineering models and vice versa. He has worked with Dr. Williams on numerous projects dating back several decades.

Chapter 1

Fraud, Lies, and Statistics

Figures don't lie, but liars do figure.

—Anonymous

As mentioned in the Preface, one of the authors (Edward E. Williams) and M. Chapman Findlay published a controversial article in 1980 titled "A Positivist Evaluation of the New Finance." It was intended to be a spoof on Milton Friedman's concept of positivism which will be a major concern in this book. They presented the paper in 1978 at an academic conference, and they knew at the time that they were venturing into treacherous waters. Nevertheless, the article was one of the most read in the journal that published it for many years. Basically, the article called into question what had been going on in academic finance for the previous two decades, i.e., the introduction of the "scientific method" to finance (or what was soon becoming "financial economics").

The metamorphosis to "science" was well along the way in economics departments by the 1960s as the old institutional professors were being replaced by statistically competent "econometricians," and so-called "armchair theorists" by mathematically trained researchers. Indeed, many an economist started down the path to being a Ph.D. mathematician or physicist only to find the work too intellectually challenging. By switching to economics, where the senior faculty and deans had no idea what you were doing, a sinecure could be established. There was a bonus as well since established mathematical theorems (both abstract and from physics) could be transformed *en masse* to create economic propositions that might work if the proper assumptions could be made.

These young economists soon took over their profession by assuming leadership roles on the editorial boards of leading academic journals. These boards governed what papers would be published and, hence, who would get the "prize" which was generally a prerequisite for a Nobel Prize in Economics. Of course the "prize" to which we refer is tenure! This is not to say that these "young Turks" (who are the old guard today, or in many cases, no longer guarding much of anything from their heavenly perches) were either unscrupulous or useless. As we will see eventually, the work of these pioneers in both economics and finance brought smart people into the professions and made changes that were, in general, more positive than negative. We will dwell on the negative, however, in most of this book.

One of the most important research "products" of these pioneers was the efficient market hypothesis (EMH). There are lots of reasons to assess the efficacy of the EMH. It has been one of the most discussed topics in financial economics. Literally thousands of papers and books have been written on the subject. Its "truth" has been debated from its inception over five decades ago when the term "random walk" first began to circulate. Indeed, some might ask, "why do we need another book on the subject?" Quite candidly, if all we proposed to do here was rehash the "is it true?" debate, another book would definitely not be in order. However, the purpose here is not simply to judge whether securities markets are efficient but to assess the history of the academic development of the notion. This is quite a different matter since the epistemological foundations of the study of finance come vividly into play.

As it turns out, even more important is the real-world impact of implicitly regarding the EMH as even an artifact of reality. Behind it all, however, are some very elementary statistical concepts and an understanding of the distinction among the notions of "certainty," "risk," and "uncertainty." Statisticians refer to "certainty" as knowing something with a 100% (1.0) chance of occurrence. It is hard to conceive of perfect certainty, at least over any reasonable span of time because we know things always change. Even the idea of the universe continuing to exist in the next instant is not a complete certainty. But over the next few seconds or so, the probability surely approaches unity (100%).

More reasonable is the concept of "risk." In this case, we know all possible outcomes of an event occurring (called an "exhaustive distribution"), and we know exactly the probability of each event. For example, if you have an "honest" (meaning correctly balanced between "heads" and "tails") two-sided coin, the probability of tossing a "head" is 50% (or 0.5). Similarly, the probability of tossing a tail is 50% (0.5). There are only two outcomes, both of which are known, and the probability of each outcome occurring is exactly 0.5. If we placed a wager on a coin toss, say I bet "heads" and you bet "tails" for a dollar, the "expected value" of the toss for me would be a 50% chance of winning (heads) and a 50% chance of losing (tails). The expected value of the toss for me would be as follows: $(0.5)(+\$1) + (0.5)(-\$1) = \$0$. By the same logic, your expected value would be the same, only reversing tails for heads.

The concept of complete "uncertainty" is much less satisfying. Here, we do not know all possible outcomes of an event transpiring much less the probabilities of each. Unfortunately, the real world is full of such uncertainty. Scientists may try to reduce the uncertainty of the earth being hit by an asteroid through empirical knowledge and calculation, but even here we are dealing with very subjective probabilities. Because uncertainty is so unacceptable and unsatisfactory to deal with, economists have attempted to cast the uncertain world into a framework of risk through constructing assumed distributions. Often the assumptions are reasonable. Sometimes they are not; and when they are not, economic theory can go down a very treacherous path. As we shall see eventually, this is precisely the path taken by the architects of the EMH.

A famous University of Chicago economist by the name of Frank Knight wrote a book called *Risk, Uncertainty, and Profit* in 1921. In his book, Professor Knight made it very clear that economists were seriously mistaken when they blurred the distinction between uncertainty and risk. John Maynard Keynes made an identical point in his *Treatise on Probability* the same year and later in his great opus, *The General Theory of Employment, Interest, and Money* (1936). Although Keynes is more generally known for his breakthrough work in what is now known as macroeconomics, he was also a very adept statistician. Keynes felt that most real-world economic phenomena could not be even grossly quantified and to try to do so could result in unbelievable analytical harm. This is true because the future of many real-world events is (and will always be) truly uncertain. It is assumed by econometricians today that Keynes lacked the computing facility to analyze large data sets. This is so, but it is also clear from the research of post-Keynesian scholars (see Paul Davidson, *Who's Afraid of John Maynard Keynes*, 2017) that even with powerful computers and lots of data, Keynes would have remained a skeptic about reducing a truly unknowable future to assumed probability distributions and, as we will see, so should we.

Three decades ago, Findlay and Williams published an article in the *Journal of Portfolio Management*

(1986) with a rather modest goal: to reintroduce the Knightian–Keynesian distinction between risk and uncertainty. Others had been making this observation in the post-Keynesian economics literature, but the finance journals long ago abandoned the distinction among uncertainty, risk, and (to a large extent) certainty. Subsequent to the publication of this article, Black Monday (1987), the Long-Term Capital Management collapse (1998), the dot.com bubble (2000), and the Enron implosion (2001) soon came to pass. There is a connection between the occurrence of these events and the blurring of the uncertainty/risk distinction which will become very clear in the pages to follow.

In any case, the 1986 Findlay and Williams article failed to persuade, so it was tried again with a different and updated approach in a later article with J. R. Thompson in the same journal (Findlay, Williams and Thompson, 2003). The essence of the argument was the same as our discussion a few paragraphs ago. "In a certain world, all future events have a single outcome, and both the events and their outcome are known (i.e., probability = 1). In a world of risk, future events can have multiple outcomes, but the outcomes and their probabilities are known (so that the probabilities of the outcomes of an event sum to 1). In an uncertain world, neither events nor outcomes are known, and assignment of probabilities is a meaningless exercise" (pp. 91–92).

Now it would seem quite reasonable to observe that we live in an uncertain world, parts of which, at our peril, we may attempt to model as (near) certain or risky. Unfortunately, modern financial economists (especially the Nobel Prize winners addressed in this book) have ceased simply to use models and have begun to believe (or, worse yet, believe in) them, almost religiously. In an uncertain world, it is unexceptional to note that markets may clear at a price, such that the movement from one clearing price to the next is essentially random (to be identified shortly as the weak form of the EMH) or that new information with obvious value implications moves price and does so rapidly (i.e., a very crude semi-strong form efficiency also to be discussed in greater detail in the pages to follow). No justification is provided for erecting a massive equation-driven model of the financial system(s), as has been done by the financial economists. This is particularly true since many of the decision-making inferences derived from these constructs have involved "betting the farm" on them (e.g., Enron). In an uncertain world, available investment alternatives' future returns cannot be described by probability distributions, much less by parameters (e.g., mean, variance, and covariance) of such distributions. Hence, there is no need for investor choice criteria expressed in such terms.

As we shall see in Chapter 2, a world of uncertainty was unacceptable to the evolving discipline of financial economics, even though methods have been derived to deal with such a world. Some years ago, Professor Williams outlined the basics of these methods in an article published in a very interesting book edited by

Paul Davidson (*Can the Free Market Pick Winners?
What Determines Investment,* 1993, pp. 83–130). This
is not the place to go into alternative procedures for
dealing with uncertainty, however. All we need to note
here is that, without considering other possibilities,
financial economists chose to substitute risk for uncertainty and ultimately push for general pricing models.
To some degree, this was due to the convenience of
having well-developed statistical techniques that could
be readily applied (see the Markowitz discussion in
Chapter 2). Tractability (the ability to get specific
mathematical results) was also a prime consideration.
As modern finance evolved, having mathematically
correct models became more important than having
less elegant but more properly descriptive explanations
of the real world.

A feature of classical economics was the notion of
"utility" — the idea that there is a desirability of income
or wealth which may not be proportional to value. It is
generally assumed to rise with wealth, but not as
rapidly. Hence, winning $100 will not provide as much
pleasure as losing $100 will provide pain. It is this fea-
ture (i.e., diminishing marginal utility) which produces
risk aversion. While diminishing marginal utility may
indeed apply to most goods individually at a point in
time (and gives rise to downward-sloping demand
curves), it is not as clear that it might apply to
the demand for all goods together over time (i.e.,
wealth) nor that consumption opportunities are the
only desirable attributes of wealth.

The organized study of risk preferences in the economics literature goes back to Professors von Neumann and Morgenstern and their famous 1944 book, *The Theory of Games and Economic Behavior*. Their interest in the subject prompted the rediscovery of Bernoulli's analysis of the St. Petersburg paradox of 1738. They formalized the axioms of expected utility analysis, leading to the proposition that the utility of a risky event was not the utility of the expected value of the event but rather the expected value of the utility of each outcome of the event. To derive an individual's utility function from which the so-called risk "indifference" curves can then be extracted is tough. Indifference means a precisely balanced trade-off between risk and return such that an investor would be "indifferent" as to the choice. To do so requires asking lottery-type questions where all the probabilities and payoffs are specified so that the expected value of the utility of each outcome can be computed. Clearly, this procedure can only apply to a world of risk. Moreover, the sorts of utility curves envisioned by economists do not explain gambling, one of the few types of pure risk situations people actually encounter.

The dilemma here is obvious. People buy insurance to avoid the pain of, say, a million dollar loss even though the probability of such a loss might be only $1/10^{th}$ of a percent. The expected value of the loss would be as follows: $(0.001)(\$1,000,000) = \$1,000$. The insurance might cost $\$1,100$ due to the expense of underwriting, profit to the insurance company, etc.

This "game" has a negative expected value of $100, but people are willing to pay to avoid a "wipe-out" type loss. The idea of a "premium" (literally what it is called in the insurance world) suggests that the purchaser will pay a price in this range of his or her "utility function" to avoid loss. Since people are willing to pay to avoid loss, it is generally posited by economists that the rational economic actor is "risk averse" and has to be compensated for assuming risk. This notion is at the heart of finance; and it is the reason, for example, that the expected return from equities should exceed those from treasury bills.

Now the same people who buy insurance will also buy lottery tickets. Say Mr. X buys a ticket to win a million dollars at a cost of $1. Assume the probability of winning the lottery is one in ten million. The expected value of the "game" is only: $(1/10,000,000)$ $(\$1,000,000) = 10$¢. Mr. X plays because the cost ($1) is nominal. Because such gambles are taken at unfair odds (the "house profit" or in the case of most lotteries the "state take"), the behavior implies "risk seeking" over this range of the purchaser's utility function. The implication here is the presence of "risk assumer" behavior (i.e., people are prepared to pay rather than get paid to take on risk). Why would a rational person pay a price exceeding the expected value of a "deal" (the lottery ticket) to become a millionaire and also pay a price exceeding the expected value of losing $1 million?

In the economics literature, earlier functions did account for gambling [see Friedman and Savage (1948) and Markowitz (1952b)]. These functions generated indifference curves which may not provide unique tangency solutions with the so-called "efficient frontiers" as developed by Harry Markowitz (1952b) and discussed in Chapter 2. Researchers came to simply assume that people had utility functions with specific properties in order to make the math work. Much of this argument is discussed in more detail in the first author's book, *Models for Investors in Real World Markets*, published by John Wiley & Sons in 2003, for interested readers. Notice here that "making the math work" ultimately became more important than providing a real-world description of how people and markets behave. This elevation of mathematical tractability became the hallmark of modern financial economics. The elegance of the model came first. The relation to reality was not so important.

One might wonder why the study of the history of financial thought makes any difference. Most economics departments quit teaching the history of thought years ago, and very few students of finance have ever read most of the articles and books we shall examine in this volume. In a way, this is a sad commentary on strictly intellectual grounds, but even for quite practical reasons, there is a lot to be learned from the evolving study of financial economics and its bastard child, the EMH.

Suppose you were a university trustee charged with at least nominal fiduciary responsibilities for the spending of the income from your university's endowment. Suppose further that it was discovered that literally billions of dollars had been spent on a "project" which turned out to be an intellectual fraud (very loosely defined) and your university had devoted large portions of its budget to underwriting some of the ·project. As part of the underwriting spending, certain professors were paid handsome sums for doing research on this endeavor and even were given leave from teaching responsibilities. Would you want to know how this happened? The President of your university made conscious decisions to regularly cut the budgets of certain departments (say in the hard sciences like Chemistry and Physics) to support the "project." Again, would you want to know how and perhaps even why this happened?

Now suppose you were responsible for providing research grants from a foundation which had proper eleemosynary goals and qualified for general tax protection at the expense of the United States Treasury. Suppose further that you had provided funding for the aforementioned "project" that turned out to be an intellectual fraud. Would you care? It should be noted that we have used the word "project" in a very general sense because there was no specific research agenda or proposal called the "EMH project." Rather, it was an evolving cascading of papers and books that robbed other quite worthy areas of research from being pursued. This was literally the case in finance and economics, but it was also true because finance department chairs, business school deans, etc., were able to convince universities, foundations, and other providers of research grants that studying the EMH was more valuable than spending precious resources elsewhere.

Advancing into another realm, suppose you were a large institutional stockholder of a publicly held corporation that was sued for billions of dollars. The corporation was sued in a class action matter that involved supposed securities fraud and the proof of the case involved assuming that the results of the previously mentioned project were scientifically determined and correct. Most definitely you would care. Even the judges (and Justices) who adjudicated these matters might care.

It is safe to say that all of the parties mentioned above (along with many others including poorly paid English professors and scientists with serious projects who were denied money due to the EMH "project" taking an undue share of tightly budgeted funding) would care. Likewise, officers, directors, and stockholders of all publicly held corporations care. Perhaps, even finance professors who argued against the EMH and had their papers ultimately rejected (resulting in not getting tenure) would also care. Most of the EMH expenditure has already taken place in the past, and there is not much one can do about past mistakes except to learn from them so as not to repeat a similar behavior.

It seems to us at this juncture that the most important area for caring is in the legal arena, as it is where the real mischief is being spread. The conservative members of the U.S. Supreme Court are market-oriented in their beliefs. Hence, it is not surprising that they would presume the stock market is efficient (simply because the conservative economists say so). But even liberal members of the Court have fallen prey to the EMH. In *Halliburton Co. v. Erica P. John Fund, Inc.*,[1] the Court unanimously upheld the "fraud on the market" (FOTM) doctrine originally found in *Basic, Inc. v. Levinson*.[2] *Basic* holds that the EMH provides that all publicly available material information, including alleged misstatements, is reflected in a security's price traded on a well-developed market. Share purchasers are relying on the assurance that the stock price is not distorted by a corporation's fraud. When this presumption is violated, FOTM permits a class action lawsuit.

Halliburton came before the Supreme Court on the matter of class certification which upheld the FOTM theory, but the case was remanded to the District Court with the requirement that the defendant (Halliburton) prove that material misstatements did not affect the market price of the stock. This task was accomplished using the event study tool (a longstanding

---

[1] *Halliburton Co. v. Erica P. John Fund, Inc. (Halliburton II)*, 134 S. Ct. 2398, 573 U.S. 258, 2403 L. Ed. 339 (2014).
[2] *Basic, Inc. v. Levinson*, 485 U.S. 224, 225, 108 S. Ct. 978, 980 L. Ed. 194 (1988).

EMH technique, with its own *JEL*[3] classification, G140); the conclusion of the case, after a protracted battle by both sides' experts (statisticians), was that the Class was certified only for the corrective disclosure of December 7, 2001, and for none of the other five dates in the original 30-month period. FOTM based on EMH was upheld, with the only real change being that plaintiffs need not prove price impact at the class certification stage, but a defendant may rebut the presumption of reliance by proving that the alleged misrepresentations did not distort the market price of the company's stock. In other words, a defendant in a securities case must have an opportunity, before a class of plaintiffs is certified, to rebut the presumption that the plaintiffs relied on the defendant's misrepresentations in purchasing stock.

Halliburton argued that progress in empirical economic research has shown market efficiency no longer tenable (a point considered at length later in this book). The Court instead found that *Basic* acknowledged the debate among economists about this and refused to endorse "any particular theory of how quickly and completely publicly available information is reflected in market price." Although the Supreme Court did keep the FOTM presumption alive, it underscored that it is only a presumption.

In August 2016, the case was again on appeal in the Fifth Circuit Court, but by December 2016,

---

[3] *Journal of Economic Research.*

Halliburton announced that it had agreed to settle for $100 million. This left the assumption of market efficiency *in limbo*. Although the empirical research alluded to by Halliburton and its experts definitely called into question the EMH, most of their arguments were based on the "market anomalies" area, which we discuss in Chapter 7. It may appear that even though the U.S. Supreme Court recognized that there was "debate" among economists, we shall soon see why there should have been no debate in the first place.

Chapter 2

The Early History of Modern Financial Economics

A man who seeks advice about his actions will
not be grateful for the suggestion that he maximize
expected utility.

— A.O. Roy

Over the past 50 years, the late Professor M. C. Findlay
(1944–2008) joined one of the authors (Edward E.
Williams) to provide a critique of the intellectual path
taken by financial economists. The late Professor J. R.
Thompson (1938–2017) joined in the task more
recently. Some of the fruits of these collaborations are
provided in this chapter.

In its early days, research in finance was essentially
taxonomic and descriptive. There was only one real academic journal at the time (the *Journal of Finance*)
although occasionally the economics journals (*American
Economic Review, Journal of Political Economy*, etc.) and

the *Journal of Business* published articles on financial topics. The *Financial Analysts Journal* produced mainly practical articles, although some were quite scholarly. The leading textbooks were institutional in character and provided long, boring almost legal descriptions on subjects such as bond indenture agreements, claims in the event of bankruptcy, etc.

It was assumed that research in finance was supposed to describe real-world phenomena (stocks, bonds, credit arrangements, and the like). The theory of the overall functioning of an economy (including the finance function) was the domain of economists. The finance function (the nature of corporations and how they raise money) was simply described by finance practitioners and professors. Why corporations exist (aside from legal considerations) and any sort of notion about a general theory of the subject was not a part of finance, although as we shall see some rudimentary propositions were put forth even early on.

Finance as an area of formal study was initially defined as the financing of corporations through the issuance of debt and equity securities. The subject was divided into two subareas: corporate finance (the study of the issuance of securities) and investments (the study of the purchase of securities). The general reasoning was that markets are best understood as institutional arrangements. The pricing of securities was accepted as inefficient by definition. A list of the earliest texts would include (in order of date published): Ripley, *Railroads: Finance and Organizations,* 1915; Dewing,

The Financial Policy of Corporations, 1919; Dewing, *Corporation Finance*, 1922; Mead, *Corporation Finance*, 1923; Gerstenberg, *Financial Organizations*, 1933; Graham and Dodd, *Security Analysis*, 1934; and Shaffner, *The Problem of Investment*, 1936. Of these, the Graham and Dodd's book became an investment classic and was carried into editions for decades. It was truly the "bible" for securities analysts for generations, and its principal author (Ben Graham, a Finance Professor at Columbia University) was a teacher and mentor to the most successful of all modern investors, Warren Buffett.

Predicates of this literature were books arguing that investment decisions were often based on irrationality. Among the more well-known ones was Charles Mackay's 1841 classic *Extraordinary Popular Delusions and the Madness of Crowds*. In 1931, F. A. Allen wrote *Only Yesterday*, a great little book about speculation in the 1920s. Keynes' (1936) *The General Theory of Employment, Interest, and Money*, particularly Chapter 12, fits into this category as well although his endeavor had a very different overall purpose. Excellent quotations from these volumes are found in Chapters 3 and 4.

Methodologically, even most economists before the mid-20th century treated their subject more or less in a descriptive fashion. To be sure, there were those like the famous Leon Walras, Vilfredo Pareto, and even Cambridge's Alfred Marshall who extensively used diagrams and equations, but economists who were mostly interested in financial subjects (the Austrian school, for example) did their analysis in English (or German, as the case might be). These economists who studied topics such as rates of return on capital and "the" rate of interest employed very elementary equations and diagrams. The Austrians (von Mises, Kirzner, etc.) did their work in English (or German). Professor Knight and Keynes (see Chapter 1) wrote mostly in English prose, but nevertheless also offered hypotheses about the way markets behave. These propositions were often not testable in a purely scientific way, but they were analytical statements nonetheless. The proof was usually casual empirical observation without employing statistical data gathering. Most writers at the time did not think "scientific" testing of these propositions could be accomplished (as perhaps, one might do in the real sciences like physics or chemistry). These were still analytical, theoretical hypotheses. After all, Keynes wrote a "general theory" which was quite analytical and which depended almost entirely on casual empiricism. Moreover, he wrote almost completely in English with very little appeal to the use of equations and diagrams.

Economics in modern times has become quite a different discipline. By the 1950s, the majority of work appearing in the economics literature was no longer merely descriptive and taxonomic, and the subject matter became broader and more theoretical in nature. Eventually, method became theory, and it was assumed that the methods employed by the physical sciences were appropriate for social studies research. Indeed, the term "studies" was replaced by "sciences" in most universities, such that the term "social science" was born. "Government" became "political science," etc. Similarly, a new branch of economics (subsequently known as "financial economics") was born. To a degree, this was the result of a doctoral dissertation written by a University of Chicago graduate student named Harry Markowitz. His work was not readily recognized as "financial economics" and even Milton Friedman, who was on the Markowitz doctoral committee, said the effort was an exercise in mathematical programming and not really economics. As it turned out, the Markowitz dissertation was summarized and subsequently published in 1952, in the only real academic finance journal. The paper was laden with diagrams and equations and really looked odd alongside the other papers in that issue of the *Journal of Finance*. One of the authors of this book (Williams) was a student at Wharton a few years after the publication of the Markowitz paper. It had begun to appear in readings books (of academic papers) by this time, and students of finance at the "better" universities were required to read the paper, although most professors had no idea how to teach it. The general instruction was, "Read it and we will discuss it later." For most of us (students at the time), later was well into Ph.D. programs where our professors still didn't know what to make of it.

In many respects, Markowitz was carrying on from the work in utility theory of Bernoulli and von Neumann/Morgenstern (Chapter 1). He included at least a discussion of the dynamic, multi-period selection problem which was an attempt to model portfolio decision-making not only at a single point in time but over time spans, conceivably to infinity. (The reader might begin to get the idea here that many financial economists actually believe the future of the world can be condensed into "forever" space.) Markowitz was trying to quantify the age-old problem of diversification which had existed since the first market for securities developed centuries ago.

In earlier years, a portfolio manager's job was to take the work of securities analysts (finding cheap stocks to buy or overpriced stocks to sell) and then determine the minimum income stream required by his (very few "hers" in those days) client(s). He would also take into account the ability of the client to take on risk. Risk was defined as a drop in asset values to the point where the client(s) might have to liquidate assets to continue having a needed income stream. The first decision to be made was the allocation among cash, bonds, and equities. In more modern times, one could add commodities, derivatives, real estate, exchange traded funds, etc. A general heuristic was to place enough of the portfolio into bonds so that interest payments plus any dividends earned on the equity allocation would meet the minimum income requirement of the client in all but the very worst years (read 1929 and subsequently). Beyond this consideration, the ratio of bonds to equities might also be varied depending upon the manager's view of the cycle (for example, less stock and more bonds at the peak of a boom). The bond portfolio would then be divided among governments, municipals (depending on the client's tax status), utilities, and railroads (now transportation), according to the perceived risk or manager's tastes. Diversification of maturity was also obtained to protect against interest rate swings and to avoid the necessity of investing large sums at an inopportune future time. The stock portfolio would be apportioned among cyclical, defensive, value and growth stocks with further "diversification" among small capitalization, middle capitalization, and large capitalization equities. In more recent times, international and emerging market holdings have been thrown into the pot. Finally, with the proportions determined, the manager would select among various securities from a list determined by securities analysts.

Employing the above sequence, the proverbial widow, heir, etc. who had funds to invest would calculate his or her income needs and the manager would fit a portfolio around those needs. Historically this meant large bond holdings with additional income generated by preferred stocks or high dividend yielding common stocks. The future growth of the portfolio (to provide increased income over time to account for inflation) would come from a selection of growth-oriented equities. On the other hand, the proverbial young business executive would generally have enough income and other assets to live without income from his portfolio. He could thus be more aggressive in his investments and allocate most of his assets to equities and growth stocks at that. Therefore, the portfolio decision for widows (at the most conservative end of the client spectrum) and young business executives (at the opposite end) were derived by the systematic application of the same decision framework to differing individual circumstances.

Institutional portfolio policies (and eventually regulations) were derived in a similar manner. Because bank assets represent the funds of depositors and life insurance companies' investments are the same for policy holders' reserves, it was felt that these institutions should have little exposure to asset price declines. Mutual fund portfolios and other similar institutional investors could shoulder a range of asset price fluctuations depending on the advertised nature of the funds. Common stock-oriented portfolios would obviously invest in equities, and these might fit the business executive profile discussed above.

The major difficulty with the approaches outlined previously was that they are based on the assumption that portfolio risk is the weighted sum of the total risk of the component securities, considered in isolation. As Markowitz demonstrated, this was simply untrue. Another unfortunate assumption of the earlier methodology was that the "cafeteria" approach to security selection ("a little of this, a little of that") resulted in efficient diversification. As Markowitz further showed, this contention was also incorrect. The impact of Markowitz's work was to change the role of the portfolio manager. Instead of depending on a list of buy, hold, and sell securities prepared by a security analyst, the "modern" portfolio manager should be concerned with statistics such as the mean, variance, and covariance of returns of particular assets with other assets. The considerations of client returns should be treated in the form of utility functions, with risk–return trade-offs being suggested by diagrams and equations, most of which few people reading this book could reproduce or even understand. Thus, it isn't far from the mark to say that, while Markowitz was theoretically correct, and the older methods were grossly over simplified and even wrong, what was proposed to take their place was almost mathematically impossible to navigate without equally gross oversimplifications.

It should be noted that today it is virtually unheard of for any client to sit down and actually figure out what one's utility functions actually look like. Moreover, at least in the original Markowitz work, the following had to be done: First, investors (or their managers) had to know all asset purchase opportunities that were available. Second, they had to combine all opportunities in various proportions to form several (or several million) hypothetical portfolios. Third, they had to compute mean returns and standard deviations of those returns for each of these portfolios. Fourth, for each return, they had to select the portfolio with the least standard deviation. Fifth, an "efficiency frontier" had to be generated for the application of the aforementioned utility indifference curves. Finally, the optimal portfolio had to be selected. In theory, this was a fairly simple notion. In practice, however, the problems posed by this process were enormous. Aside from computing the means and standard deviations for each security to be analyzed, it was also necessary to estimate the covariance for each security with every other security. For just 1,000 securities, the number of covariances is greater than half a million. Furthermore, to follow the above suggested method, one would need to compute the parameters of a very large number of portfolios. Even if we limited portfolio holdings to a minimum of 1% of each security (100 securities in each portfolio), the number of possible portfolios would be: $1,000!/[(900!)(100!)]$. Note that the exclamation marks aren't there for emphasis, they mean factorial. That is, for even the smallest number in the equation (100), the factorial would be: $(100)(99)(98)...(1)$. In itself this is a huge number. The total number of portfolios would be 6.4×10^{139}, much more than all the proverbial elementary physics particles in the universe. Even with the aid of modern computers, this is a very difficult task. In Markowitz's day, it was impossible.

Thus, Markowitz proposed a method for simplifying this task in a 1956 paper, but the math was still daunting. Interestingly, the title of the paper, "The Optimization of a Quadratic Function Subject to Linear Constraints," reveals that the work was really more mathematics than finance or even economics. Note here the attempt to use a fairly old calculation method (mathematical programming) is fitted to the problem at hand. This shows how people principally trained in math (who could not have gotten Ph.D.'s in the subject) simply moved their tool kit over to the social "sciences" to get doctorates and publications! It is also of note that this 1956 paper was published in the *Naval Research Logistics Quarterly*. Just what interest the Navy had in utility functions remains anybody's guess. In some respects, it may be said that Markowitz had a great insight but even with lots of simplifying (and sometimes ridiculous) assumptions, the work required to perform the calculations prevented "modern portfolio theory" from being much more than a financial economist's pipe dream. We shall return to some more simplifying methods shortly, but we shall see that, Nobel Prizes notwithstanding, these methods were only modest improvements on Markowitz's impractical theory.

As the author of the seminal paper on modern portfolio theory, Markowitz built his work around certain definitions and assumptions. To him, they were reasonable for the work he set out to do. However, most of these definitions and assumptions have continued in place and remained more or less unchallenged for over six decades. Markowitz assumed that security returns could be described by what statisticians call an "intertemporally independent normal distribution." Such a distribution is unhelpfully called a "bell curve" in common parlance. It has specific properties such as a mean (a measure of central tendency) and variance (as a measure of dispersion around the central tendency). Markowitz further assumed that the mean (as a measure of expected value) was "good" but that the variance (as a measure of risk) was "bad," such that the investment problem involved a trade-off of the one against the other. This was basically the point at which variance of return became the measure of risk in the finance literature.

As Findlay, Williams and Thompson pointed out in the *Journal of Portfolio Management* (2003, p. 93):

> "The real insight of Markowitz is that return aggregates but that risk does not. In other words, the expected return (mean) of the portfolio will be a dollar-weighted average of the returns (means) of the individual securities, but the risk (variance) of the portfolio will only be such an average in the limiting case where all of the securities' returns are perfectly correlated with each other. In all other cases, it will be lower.
>
> Thus it could be said that Markowitz provided a statistical definition of the benefits of diversification. If the securities are uncorrelated with each other, a large number of small investments will produce a near-riskless portfolio of investments (even though the investments are individually risky).
>
> Markowitz then defines another concept of *efficiency* as that portfolio that has the highest return for a given level of risk, or, equivalently, the lowest risk for a given return. The set of efficient portfolios was called the efficient frontier, and it was argued that all rational, and risk-averse investors would select a portfolio from that set.
>
> A more explicit assumption of a world of risk would be hard to imagine."

Interestingly, another Nobel Prize winner, James Tobin (1958), probably produced the first actual risk–return diagram in which alternative portfolios are graphed against indifference curves (i.e., all points having the same expected utility), where the optimal solution is the point of tangency of the opportunity set with the highest indifference curve. The article was framed in terms of "liquidity preference" which Keynes dealt with extensively in both *The Treatise on Probability* (1921) and in *The General Theory of Employment, Interest, and Money* (1936). Keynes made his arguments as part of an uncertainty case whereas Tobin headed down the slippery slope of statistical risk. Ultimately, the older Keynesian version, while not as mathematically tractable, appears to comport with real-world facts more than Tobin's (and Markowitz's) "more sophisticated" versions (see Davidson, 2018). Paul Samuelson, who in 1970 was the first American to win the Nobel Prize in Economic Sciences, provided a novel proof of diversification in his 1967 article, "General Proof that Diversification Pays."

A few years ago, two economists named Franco Modigliani and Merton Miller (MIT and Chicago, respectively, and also Nobel Prize winners) published a paper (1958) which in many respects was even more important methodologically than Markowitz's work. Modigliani and Miller (henceforward MM) suggested a way to analyze financial problems that mirrored the equilibrium models that had been percolating in economics for many years. The MM paper (which appeared not in a finance journal but the *American Economic Review*) dealt with capital structure issues. Historically, it was argued that firms have a cost of debt capital (bonds, etc.) and a cost of equity capital (stock, retained earnings, etc.). In general, as debt is added to a company's financial structure, the cost of both debt and equity rises due to the increase in riskiness posed by debt. However, debt is comparatively cheaper than equity and may offer a tax advantage (being generally deductible from corporate income taxes, whereas dividend payments are not). Thus, the combining of debt and equity in reasonable amounts can reduce the weighted average cost of capital (WACC) to a company. For example, suppose a firm has zero debt and a 10% cost of equity. Its WACC would also be 10%. At a 50% debt and 50% equity capital structure, debt might cost 6% and equity 12%. If the company was in the 21% tax bracket (t), its after-tax cost of debt would be: $(1 - t) (6\%) = (0.79) (6\%) = 4.7\%$. Its WACC would be: $(0.5) (4.7\%) + (0.5) (12\%) = 8.3\%$. Over a range (say from 40–60% debt), the WACC might be more or less the same 8.3% (as costs and weights moved around). A lower debt load might result in a higher overall WACC as might one in excess of 60%. Obviously, the lower the WACC, the higher the enterprise value of the firm and vice versa.

The subject of capital structure was long considered in finance even by the 1950s. For example, Professor Ezra Solomon of Stanford used the term "optimal capital structure" in his advanced corporation finance textbook (1963) to describe the phenomenon. The idea was even broached much earlier by J. B. Williams who called it the "Law of Conservation of Investment Value" in

1938. Williams discussed its implications and discarded what ultimately looked a lot like what MM proposed in a paragraph! MM introduced an "arbitrage proof" to argue that there was no "optimal capital structure." It was their position in the *American Economic Review* paper that, given two firms with the same business risk and the same operating income, each firm would have the same value regardless of the method of financing. Consider two firms the same in all respects but capital structure. Assume both have an operating income of $1,000 which will continue in perpetuity. Firm A is completely financed by equity and firm B is financed by both debt and equity. If firm A has a cost of equity of 8%, the enterprise value of A would be given by: $1,000/0.08 = $12,500. Firm B has interest payments of $200 with the remaining $800 of operating income going to the equity holders. If B's cost of debt is 4%, the value of its debt (ignoring the tax advantage, which MM did by the way, and we will come back to later) would be $200/0.04 = $5,000. If B had a cost of equity capital of 10% (higher than A's due to the added risk factor of using debt), the value of its equity would be $800/0.10 = $8,000. Thus, the total value of B would be $5,000 + $8,000 = $13,000. MM argued this was not possible and that the price of B's stock was too high.

We will go through the rest of the MM argument shortly, but we should first pause and reflect on just how simple the model postulated is. The two firms are identical (try to find these in the real world). The income streams are identical (ditto), and both will enjoy these streams forever (ditto again). MM and subsequent researchers in financial economics maintained these simplifications since they were needed in order to do any sort of analysis. Hence, one of the first methodological building blocks of what Findlay and Williams (1980) later called the "New Finance" was the reduction of reality to easily manipulated but unrealistic scenarios. This was considered altogether proper due to an earlier argument by the famous Milton Friedman who maintained in his 1953 book *Essays in Positive Economics* that even apparently absurd assumptions could be made so long as the results of the analysis in question were empirically realistic. Now however one might feel about the macroeconomic debate of Friedman vs. Keynes, one should be forewarned that Keynes built his arguments on assumptions that at least seemed to comport with reality. Professor Friedman didn't think this was necessary and much of the nonsense we discuss in this book comes from the Friedmanian adoption of positivism. As we shall see, his view came to permeate virtually all future research in financial economics and is the reason so much of it is flawed. (As an interesting aside, an important post-Keynesian economist, Paul Davidson, stated with regard to Friedman's methods, "If the facts and the theory don't match, too bad for the facts!")

It may seem that we are spending a lot of time discussing the details of an article that appeared 60 years ago, but the MM paper is the cornerstone method of everything that follows. One has to grasp the essentials of their argument to understand the far more complex edifice that follows it. This is especially true as the MM work is fairly transparent and can be illustrated with simple numerical examples. Later research becomes far more mathematical and harder to fathom for those who are not trained economists. Indeed, one of the advantages of conducting business in a foreign (to most business people) language is that it is hard to argue with what you can't comprehend. Higher mathematics is this language and we suspect few people awarding Nobel Prizes (unless they are card-carrying members of the "Club" and hence biased) have any idea about what is actually contained in the work for which these prizes are awarded.

Let us return to the actual assumptions made by MM. First, they assumed that firms can be grouped into homogeneous business classes. This means that firms exist that are exact carbon copies of each other. Of course, no such grouping can be found in actuality; but if one accepts the Friedmanian concept of positivism, that doesn't matter. MM's second assumption was that investors are perfectly rational. Boy, that makes a lot of sense to anyone who has ever put a dime in the securities markets, doesn't it? Third, they assumed securities markets operate under conditions of perfect competition where there are no transactions costs. This may be closer to a reality today, but it certainly was not in 1958, when the NYSE enforced strict 100 share round lot commissions that could be well over 1% of the value of a transaction. Finally, it was assumed that there were no corporate income taxes. Really? What planet did they live on?

The math of the MM argument is not hard to follow, but it does require one to refrain from laughing out loud. Let's return to the example of firm A and B above. Recall that they argued that the price of B's stock was too high. Indeed, they suggested that B is only worth $7,500 and that the cost of equity capital to B should be 10.67% rather than 10%, and in "equilibrium" shareholders will sell B's stock until it reaches a value of $7,500. Be patient while we go through MM's belief that this is so. First, assume Jones owns 1% of the stock of firm B. It would pay Jones to sell his stock and buy A's stock. If he sold his stock, the proceeds would be: (0.01) ($8,000) = $80. Now Jones could assume the same risk associated with his investment in B by engaging in what MM called "homemade leverage." Thus, firm B was financed 5/13 by debt, whereas firm A has no debt. For Jones to have the same risk as he had when he owned B, he should borrow $50. Jones' "personal" capital structure mix ($50 debt and $80 equity) would be the same as firm B's. With the proceeds from the sale B plus the $50 loan, Jones could now buy $130/$12,500 or 1.04% of A. The question would be: Why would Jones sell B and buy A? According to MM, the answer was easy. If Jones held B, his return would be: (1%) ($800) = $8. If he sells, borrows, and buys A, however, his return would be: (1.04%) ($1,000) = $10.40. From this return, he must pay an interest of 4% on his debt, or (4%) ($50) = $2. Nevertheless, his gross return from holding A is $8.40, which is larger than the return would be if he held B. Thus, he would sell A and buy B.

The impact of many stockholders selling B and buying A would reduce the price of B until returns were equalized. Since the appropriate return for an unleveraged equity in this example was assumed to be 8%, the price of A would not rise. When the value of stock B declined to $7,500, equilibrium would be reached. To see why this is the case, let us return to the earlier example. If Jones sold B, his proceeds would be: (1%) ($7,500) = $75. He would borrow $50 since this is the same 5/12.5 debt to equity ratio mix evidenced by firm B. His total of $125 would buy $125/$12,500 or 1% of A. His return if he held B would be: (1%) ($800) = $8. There would be no advantage in selling B and buying A at this point. Thus, in equilibrium, the value of A ($12,500) equals the value of B ($7,500 + $5,000) = $12,500.

By this point, the reader is probably exasperated by all of the explicit assumptions (and required transactions) for this to make any sense. However, there are even more ridiculous assumptions implicitly made in the analysis. First, MM maintained that markets are perfect, investors are rational, and investors will engage in "home-made" arbitrage. This is crucial to the MM conclusions. There is no guarantee that some or any investor(s) will so engage. Furthermore, even if investors wished to behave as MM suggested, there are institutionally imposed restrictions to prevent such behavior. Federal Reserve margin requirements, for example, limit the amount of "home-made" leverage which investors may assume. Lending institutions also place roadblocks to prevent the process from working. One of the authors borrows against a stock with a 50% debt/50% equity ratio. His bank will only lend about 25% on the equity, making it impossible to duplicate the corporation's financial structure. Also, there is every reason to believe that the borrowing rate paid by investors would be greater than that of the underlying corporation. As such, there would be a clear preference for corporate rather than personal borrowing. Moreover, it seems likely that the presence of transaction costs such as brokerage fees plus the possible loss of interest deductions for tax purposes by individuals (in the real world, interest deductions for investments are allowed only up to investment income with a carry forward of the unused amount) would reduce the practicality of the arbitrage process. Finally, it should be pointed out that the personal risk assumed by the investor in "home-made" arbitrage is really greater than the indirect risk incurred by owning stock of a leveraged company. Whereas the corporation is protected by limited liability, the individual is not.

When one considers the specific cost functions implicit in the MM analysis, further problems arise. As leverage increases, MM agree that both the cost of debt and equity will rise as well. In the early stages of increased leverage, because of the weighting arrangements, the WACC may remain constant even though both component costs are rising. However, the point will eventually be reached where the cost of equity capital must fall if the cost of debt continues to rise. This makes absolutely no sense. Why would stockholders be willing to accept lower returns as the risk position of the corporation increases? This factor alone would tend to cause the cost of equity capital to rise (perhaps at an increasing rate) and the WACC would be forced up. Recognizing this, MM argued that some investors will become risk seekers (gamblers) at this point, and the cost of equity will fall. It seems more than a bit contrived that all of the sudden gamblers will appear out of nowhere just in time to save the MM analysis when before all investors were assumed to be rational risk avoiders who had to be compensated (rather than paying) for additional risk!

Another embarrassment for MM was their "empirical test." They took a sample of companies, calculated their leverage positions, and computed their costs of debt and equity (hence the WACC) for each. The empirical results demonstrated their theory that the WACC was invariant with capital structure. There was one big problem, however. In the real world, it clearly pays to have to have all interest paid by the corporation (and none by investors) in order to minimize the effects of corporation double taxation. They ultimately admitted such in a *mea culpa* note, but it surprised most practitioners (and even a few professors such as Stanford's Ezra Solomon) that the MM article made it through the supposedly "blind" review process of the extremely prestigious *American Economic Review*. The problem was that most of the reviewers had no more knowledge about very important institutional arrangement than did MM. The institutional professors remaining in finance did know these facts, but within a decade they would be replaced by theoreticians like MM! As a final point, it should be observed that the so-called "empirical test" of MM was poorly conceived and constructed. The sort of statistical sloppiness evidenced should not be forgiven for a Statistics 101 student, let alone two eminent economists who both ultimately won the Nobel Prize in Economics.

Chapter 3

The Birth of the Efficient Market Hypothesis

We can easily represent things as we wish them to be.

— Aesop

The seeds for the EMH were germinated by a modest effort by Harry Roberts (*Journal of Finance*, 1959) who was a statistician at the University of Chicago at the time. Roberts' paper posited the following: (1) Movements in stock prices conform to a normal (bell curve) distribution, (2) random selections may be made from such a distribution, and (3) the results may be added to an arbitrary starting price. From this Roberts noted that the results looked a lot like the DJIA over time (for the interested reader, the process is described in mathematical detail in Thompson, Williams and Findlay, *Models for Investors in Real World Markets*, 2003).

Roberts' ideas formally go back to Louis Bachalier's 1900 doctoral dissertation *Theorie de la Speculation* and Holbrook Working's research on commodity prices in the 1920s. These earlier works were more or less forgotten by the 1950s, and Roberts' article prompted a great interest in what was soon to be called "The Random Walk Hypothesis." A plethora of papers and books (and a gold mine of doctoral dissertations) followed over the next decade.

The purpose of this line of research was to attack the so-called technical analysts who believed that there were patterns in stock price movements. Technical analysis was a staple of research going back to the Dow Theory and earlier. The Dow Theory was developed in the late 19th century by Charles Dow. It maintains that "signals" can be used to identify stock price trends. Charles Dow was part owner as well as editor of *The Wall Street Journal* until his death in 1902. He regularly wrote editorials that revealed the essence of his views and speculation.

Technical analysis was generally considered a supplement or even substitute for fundamental analysis which maintained that stocks should be analyzed using economic and accounting data such as the revenues, profits, etc. of a company. Fundamental analysis was the core of Benjamin Graham's view of security analysis, where income statements and balance sheets were pored over to find "undervalued" or "overvalued" stocks. Not coincidentally, Warren Buffett still follows his old Columbia University mentor (Graham) in this method of buying and selling stocks.

Hard-core technical analysts (or "chartists" as they were often called) were so convinced that their methods worked that millions of dollars of investment research was spent doing these procedures. Most Wall Street firms employed technical analysts at the time (and many still do) because of the following of retail customers of the chartists recommendations. Indeed, an early computer model was developed at the Wharton School that was deemed to be so good that the institutional investors using it agreed with the federal agencies not to exceed certain purchasing limits.

Notwithstanding the claims of the chartists, numerous academic papers followed Roberts' work. Many of these were carried in a book by Paul Cootner of MIT (1964). The authors of these works argued that the "price patterns" found by the chartists were merely Brownian motion (statistical noise) with no real economic impact. Cootner, for example, argued that "If any substantial group of buyers thought prices were too low, their buying power would force up the price. The reverse would be true for the sellers. Except for appreciation due to earnings retention, the conditional expectation of tomorrow's price, given today's price, is today's price. In such a world, the only price changes that would occur are those that result from new information. Since there is no reason to expect that information to be nonrandom in appearance, the period-to-period price changes should be random movements, statistically independent of one another" (Cootner, 1964, p. 232). Cootner was describing a martingale, which is a stochastic process $S(t)$ which has the property that $S(t+x$, given past$) = S(t)$ for all positive x. Thus, the best estimate of tomorrow's price of a stock is today's price.

By the early 1970s, most finance professors were convinced that there was no way to make above average returns by examining stock price time series. However, technical problems arose with the Random Walk Hypothesis even as Cootner posited it in 1964. The first had to do with the conversion of price patterns to returns (changes in prices plus dividends). In technical statistical terms, return distributions appeared to have tails "too fat" to be normal (e.g., Stable Paretian, with characteristic exponent of around 1.7 rather than 2). This invalidates one of the key assumptions of the random walk hypothesis. A second problem was what to do with the economic fact of earnings retentions. Unless corporate managers were completely stupid and consistently earn nothing from reinvested (in the business) earnings, one would expect stock prices to rise over time. These technical problems were "solved" (see Cootner, 1964) by weakening the returns assumption to a martingale with a constant (but not necessarily zero) mean and a symmetric (but not necessarily normal) distribution. Price was assumed to follow a submartingale (with a constant or rising mean) where a submartingale has the property that $S(t+x$, given past$)$ is equal to or greater than $S(t)$ for all positive x. Simply put, the best estimate of tomorrow's price of a stock is today's price adjusted for the expectation of future earnings per share due to the retention of earnings.

(*Note*: "This tendency to redesign and remake assumptions to fit the circumstances became a hallmark of the new 'scientific' revolution in finance." (Williams, 2011))

Since the purpose of the Random Walk literature was to discredit technical analysts who were deemed charlatans *prima facia* by the newly emerging financial economists, it was fairly easy to overcome the technical obstacles. Price movements assuming a submartingale was a rather short-term phenomenon and depended far more on variances and serial correlation than whether the underlying mean was zero or modestly positive. The real importance of this literature, however, was to set the stage for the emergence of the efficient markets hypothesis which is the principal topic of this book.

The essence of the evolution of the EMH was the reaction of so-called "free market" economists to the Keynesians who took over the discipline of economics after the Second World War. A small group of what are now called "neoclassical" economists continued to believe in the older price theory-driven microeconomics that Keynes had sought to destroy. The neoclassical scholars believed many markets (goods and services, wages, capital, etc.) were fairly competitive, and some approached being "perfectly competitive." In general, a perfectly competitive market is one where there are many buyers and sellers such that no single participant can influence price, where information is available at no cost to all market participants, where there are no "entry barriers" to those who wish to participate in the market, where there is a homogeneous product or service in the examined market, where common expectations are shared by all market participants, and where there are no taxes or transactions costs to deal in the market.

Now, of course, no one really believed all of the above conditions prevailed in any real-world market, but some markets might be reasonably "efficient" even if they were not perfectly competitive. What dawned on many neoclassical economists was that the market for securities perhaps came closest to satisfying the perfectly competitive model. The random walk work seemed to be a good foundation on which to resurrect the old pre-Keynesian price theory models, so a part of the battle was joined here. Other conflicts took place in the more general economics literature of course and about at this same time. Not coincidentally, the leading neoclassical economist at the time was Professor Milton Friedman; and the "Chicago School" was leading the charge in the anti-Keynesian effort. Thus, the University of Chicago Economics Department was at the fore-front, but not far behind was the University of Chicago Business School (now the Booth School) which began to be populated by economists like future Nobel Laureate Eugene Fama.

Fama (1965, 1970) is usually credited with general-izing the random walk notion of the EMH, with weak, semi-strong, and strong-form versions. Weak-form efficiency was the random walk hypothesis. Semi-strong efficiency assumed stock prices reflected all publicly available information. Strong-form efficiency assumed that, since institutions could not "beat the market" over long periods of time, no one could. Thus, new information that became available about a stock (bond, etc.) would be quickly (and without bias) impounded into the price of that stock (bond, etc.). Moreover, it was contended for many years that the market would neither exceed nor be short of the "correct" price. (It should be noted here that the "mean-reversion" literature to be discussed later had not been contemplated at this point.) Thus, by the time investor X learned of the new information, Mr. Market had already impounded it into the market price.

Author Edward E. Williams relates the following recollection:

> "Once again, as a ring-side participant in these developments, I was attending a cocktail party at the home of my friend and colleague, M. C. Findlay (to whom this book is dedicated) in 1974. At the time, Findlay was Chairman of the Finance Department at the University of Southern California, and he was busily recruiting newly minted Ph.D.'s from the University of Chicago (mostly students of Fama's). One young assistant professor of finance and I struck up a conversation about the EMH. At the time, I was a senior officer at the death care company Service Corporation International. (Disclosure: I have been associated with SCI for over 45 years and have been on its Board of Directors for much of that time.) The trough of the stock market collapse of 1974 was

imminent. Our (SCI's) stock had plummeted from 25 3/4 per share to about 2 5/8 (in the old days, share prices were quoted in fractions, generally 1/8 of a point, rather than pennies). I told the young assistant professor that our earnings per share for the past year was $1.10, our book value was about $10 per share, and our liquidating value was probably double that due to our large real estate holdings. How on earth in an 'efficient market' could we be selling for a price-to-earnings multiple of two, a huge discount (75%) from book value, and an even larger one from liquidation value? I further stated that all this was public information and as an insider I was baffled by these numbers. The young professor merely responded that 'the market knows more than you do.' I said I planned on buying the stock at the present level, and he replied it was worth only what today's market said it was worth. I bought it anyway, and the present dividend per share *per quarter* (adjusted for stock splits) is about one and one half times what I paid for those shares. The young professor elected not to buy, I assume."

Now, of course, one might make the case that market collapses occur with some regularity. The 1929 crash could have been forecasting the Great Depression (although some economists say it was the other way around). Crashes throughout the 1930s, 1940s, etc. all have occurred without the world coming to an end. The same was true of 1974, despite the oil embargo and subsequent bout of inflation. Indeed, by the 1987 crash, some EMH "true believers" were already throwing in the towel and redefining the EMH (see chapters to follow). This is fortunate in that little additional theoretical work had to be done to address the *dot.com* crash of 2000–2002 and the financial crisis of 2008–2009. In any case, the market has always been a poor forecaster of the economy. As Nobel Laureate Paul Samuelson used to say, "The market has forecasted nine of the last four recessions we have had."

In the first author's textbook over four decades ago (1974), he and Findlay followed Fama's line and catalogued the three forms of efficiency. Similarly, the same framework was analyzed in a paper by him and Professor Findlay (Findlay and Williams, 2000–2001). We cite it here since it remains one of the best historical definitions available.

> "With weak form efficiency, the information set is limited to past share price (and, perhaps, volume) data. The implication is that any information about future price movements contained in past price movements is already reflected in the current price. Technical analysis of the stock market...hence, is a waste of time.
>
> Under semi-strong efficiency, all publicly available information is impounded in stock prices. In this case, fundamental analysis (such as that purportedly undertaken by securities analysts) is useless. From a philosophical perspective, at least regarding public information, any search for a second value (e.g., fundamental value, true value, just price, etc.) to compare with market price in order to determine

whether a stock is 'cheap' or 'dear' is wrongheaded. Either there are no cheap or dear stocks or they cannot be discerned from public information.

Under strong-form efficiency, all information is considered including private information. If this condition held, even insiders could not trade for a profit" (pp. 182–183).

It was the general opinion of financial economists by the early 1970s that the weak form of the EMH stood without further investigation. Many continued to argue that, because institutional investors could rarely beat the market for long periods of time, the strong form might apply; therefore, index funds rather than mutual funds should be the investment of choice for most individual investors. This has been the consistent view of Berton Malkiel in his numerous editions of *A Random Walk Down Wall Street*.

Although the weak tests of capital market efficiency dealt with the inability to make profitable predictions of future prices from past prices, the semi-strong tests attempted to prove that prices reflect all available information. Most investigators sought to demonstrate that new information results in a rapid adjustment to a new equilibrium price that, by implication, is taken to demonstrate the price at any time must reflect all available information. Specifically, the tests have taken events such as announcements of stock splits, earnings, dividends, interest rate changes, and so on, and studied (1) how rapidly a price adjustment was made and

(2) whether the price adjustment was an unbiased evaluation of the information (such that the subsequent adjustments were as likely to be in one direction as the other). The results of the tests seemed to confirm that price adjustments occur rather quickly after the first public announcement of the information, implying that at least a significant portion of the market receives and interprets the information quickly. It could then be argued that the initial price adjustment has been generally found to be unbiased. A price trend caused by the slow spread and interpretation of new information could result in a profitable return for swift action; that such a trend does not occur is one of the foundations of EMH research.

Just how all the "testing" was done will be addressed in Chapter 6. For the time being, the reader should be warned that "scientists" who start out with a preconceived view of the world often come to conclusions consistent with their beliefs. When the so-called "scientists" are "social scientists" (rather than biologists, chemists, physicists, etc.), one should really be concerned about the prior (before the experiment) views of those doing the testing.

Thompson, Williams and Findlay (2003, p. 112) argue along these lines as follows:

> "The rise of the 'social sciences' as academic disciplines played an important role in the intellectual history of the EMH. The relationship of such areas of study as sociology, anthropology, psychology,

political science, and economics with the 'hard' sciences (physics, chemistry, etc.) at most universities was often difficult and occasionally adversarial in the past century. Originally, the social 'sciences' were deemed to be rather soft subjects which offered taxonomy rather than 'proof' or 'hypothesis testing' as their principal means of inquiry. In order to become more academically acceptable, the social sciences adopted the paradigm of the natural sciences as they began to gather 'empirical' data and apply statistical methods to analyze these data. As the softest of the social sciences, business was looked upon with disdain by other disciplines which often had ill-concealed doubts about the intellectual merit of business study and whether it really belonged on a university campus. Comparisons with business colleges (i.e., proprietary operations that taught bookkeeping, typing, etc.) were often made. It was perhaps not by chance that when Harvard established its business school, it located it across the Charles River from the rest of the campus."

In this environment, a symbiotic relationship developed. The business schools needed affiliation with academic institutions, and it didn't take long for university presidents (and university trustee boards) to figure out that business schools could bring in a ton of money. This money could be used to support English, history, philosophy, etc. departments that were drags on university budgets. Professor Williams remembers how this took place at Rice University.

"The business school raised its own money to build a building. Meanwhile, the more left-wing faculty members in the social sciences and humanities schools strongly objected to Rice having a business school in the first place. Even Rice's president at the time (an eminent chemist) thought business schools were unnecessary and said so at a seminar I attended where he pointed out that he ran a chemistry department, was a dean, and became president of a major university without benefit of going to any business or management school. On the other hand, he was presented with a major gift to start a business school and just couldn't turn down the money. The business school (originally called a school of administration) was endowed and then built the aforementioned building (once again to the howls of liberal arts and humanities professors). The business school grew and soon needed another new building. A new president said the money could be raised (again) but only by permission of the president. The price for permission was to give the old building (really not so old) back to Rice for its general purposes. These included providing nice offices for the English Department. Indeed, my old corner office was soon occupied by one of the howlers who had a totally revised view of the business school hence forward."

As Thompson, Findlay and Williams (2003, p. 113) point out:

"Many of the basic disciplines which business schools applied (e.g., economics, psychology, etc.)

had already declared themselves 'sciences' and as mentioned above were beginning to apply the 'scientific method' to their respective areas of inquiry. The answer to the 'B' school dilemma became apparent: trade your peddler's cart for a smock! The business school disciplines thus became social sciences. Finance became financial economics. Personnel management became behavioral science, etc. Being based upon a tautology (i.e., assets = liabilities + net worth), the transformation was not easy for accounting (imagine arithmetic as an 'experimental science'), but academic accountants borrowed heavily from finance and economics to give accounting the aura of 'science.' Of course, it was never demonstrated anywhere that the scientific paradigm was appropriate for these disciplines; it was simply and conveniently adopted."

We shall soon see how "business as a science" played a major role not only in the development of the EMH but also selling it as a veritable truth for many years. Cracks in the edifice appeared, as we shall see in the upcoming chapters, but it remains (even under dispute) as one of the major contributions of research in the "social sciences." President G. H. W. Bush once called certain theories in economics "voodoo" economics. He might as well have been talking about the EMH!

Chapter 4

Earlier Views of Market Efficiency

You ought never to take your little brother's chewing gum away from him by main force; it is better to rope him in with the promise of the first two dollars and a half you find floating down the river on a grindstone. In the artless simplicity natural to his time of life, he will regard it as a perfectly fair transaction. In all ages of the world this eminently plausible fiction has lured the obtuse infant to financial ruin and disaster.

— Mark Twain

As we observed in Chapter 3, under semi-strong efficiency all publicly available information is supposed to be impounded in stock prices. As a consequence, the economic and financial analysis of securities is useless. A stock (bond, etc.) is "worth" what its present market price is. This always seemed an odd notion to the many people who earn a living examining corporate financial statements, talking to management, and generally trying to understand and determine the fundamental value of securities. The essence of the securities analyst was (and is) to look at present market prices in order to determine whether a security is correctly valued, under-valued, or overvalued.

At the other end of the spectrum, most academic financial economists continue to maintain that the Warren Buffetts of the world are a rare breed. They argue that, although some investors think that funda-mental analysis may hold the key to beating the market, in reality, stock markets are intrinsic-value, random-walk phenomena. As a result, most fundamental analysts will not be able to beat the market. Only a very few experts who uncover hard-to-detect data will be able to earn above market returns, and it takes years of hard work to become such an expert. Moreover, it is unlikely that any particular person will be able to consistently discover such data. In light of efficient market evidence, one may reflect upon the work required to analyze and select securities and ask: "Why bother?"

The answer will be clear after the reader finishes this book. At this point, we should disclose our personal biases. First, we do believe that security analysis is a necessary task for every investor. There is no other way that one can make determinations of risk and return. Even if it is impossible to gain above-average rewards, forecasts of expected risk–return relationships are required for all but the most simple-minded decision algorithms. Second, we would argue that portfolio analysis is also a required activity if one is to decide in a rational framework which securities should be purchased, kept, or sold. Although some aspects of portfolio theory (especially the Markowitz approach) remain fairly abstract, operational decisions can be made using the methods employed by real-world portfolio managers. In addition, the rational investor must be able to determine his or her personal risk preferences in order to make proper selections. Finally, the way the capital markets price assets is still not perfectly known. We shall address the reasons why subsequently, but for the time being it should be noted that no really correct models exist in theoretical finance without making fairly ridiculous assumptions.

There is one point on which most people agree, however: Every individual who has more money than he or she needs for current consumption is potentially an investor. Whether surplus funds are placed in a bank at a guaranteed rate of interest or used to invest in an oil well, an investment decision must be made. These choices may be made wisely or foolishly, but the intelligent investor will seek a reasonable, consistent approach to managing one's money. The best method for many is simply to turn their funds over to someone else for management, or do as the EMH advocates suggest and buy index funds (*a la* Malkiel). A significant number of investors do indeed follow this policy, and it is quite likely the correct decision for them. Others, however, manage their own money or even become professionals and manage other people's. These folks clearly do not subscribe to the EMH. Mysteries about getting rich quickly may not be found, of course; and if such secrets existed, it is doubtful that anyone would be willing to reveal them. In any case, there are systematic procedures for making decisions that we believe can enable the intelligent investor to achieve solid performance. We will grant that there is generally a positive correlation between the returns one expects from an investment and the amount of risk that is assumed. Thus, decisions must be made that reflect the ability and desire of the investor to assume risk.

As has been observed elsewhere, (Thompson, Williams and Findlay, 2003, p. 2):

> "Although intelligence is about the only important requisite for any kind of decision making, there are other traits that may be helpful to the money manager. In particular, a certain amount of scientific curiosity may be very important to successful investors. By scientific curiosity we do not mean knowledge or even interest in disciplines generally considered 'science,' such as biology or chemistry, although the scientifically trained analyst may have an advantage in scrutinizing the stocks of high-technology companies. Rather, scientific curiosity refers to the systematic pursuit of understanding. An investor should be willing to take the time and spend the energy to know himself and his environment.
>
> It is unfortunately true that many otherwise successful people make poor investors simply because

they do not have a logical investment policy. They have only vague objectives about what they want (such as 'capital appreciation' or 'safety of principal'), and they often substitute general impressions for solid fact gathering. How many highly competent doctors, for example, go beyond the recommendations of their brokers (friends, relatives, or patients) when selecting a security? How many business people take the time to familiarize themselves with the income statements and balance sheets of the firms in which they hold stock?"

Professional portfolio managers often make decisions that are not based on a well-researched, documented effort to uncover investments that others have not discovered. Of course, a doctor may not have the time or knowledge to make sound investment decisions and the business executive or entrepreneur may be too occupied with his or her own company to do the required due diligence. If so, these individuals should not attempt to manage their own money. The professional manager who bases decisions on what one "feels" the market will do, however, is being negligent. Although knowledge of what other managers are doing may be important and an experienced person's market "feel" may be superior to any professor's theoretical model, too often even the professional tends to substitute rumor and hunch for sound analysis and thorough investigation. Lawsuits for negligence, however, are increasingly common and can undo a lifetime of investment experience.

The sophisticated investor needs to be reasonably versed in mathematics and statistics. In this book, a general perspective is provided for those who are somewhat hazy on these subjects. Our generalizations are not intended as introductory expositions to the investor who has never heard of compound interest or a standard deviation, but they should serve as an adequate guide for those who have a basic knowledge of the subject. For the reader who is totally unfamiliar with these subjects, we suggest that other books be read as a starting point (e.g., *Investments for Dummies*, etc.) before you wade further into why the EMH was a fraud on the market.

As can be seen, our biases tend toward the anti-EMH position. This is the view of the market that has long been held by most investors, and the whole profession of security analysis is founded on it as we observed above. From the early first edition of Graham and Dodd's famous book *Security Analysis* (1934) down to the present, investors have tried to identify "cheap stocks" to buy, "correctly priced stocks" to hold, and "overpriced stocks" to sell. The EMH assumes, however, that the presence of so many market participants trying to find "cheap" stocks and "dear" stocks (to sell short) makes it impossible for any one such participant to outperform the general market consistently. Of course, as the economy expands and corporate profits rise, it may be possible to make money in the stock market; but according to the EMH, it is not reasonable to expect to earn more than risk-adjusted market returns over the long run.

To a degree, the EMH hypothesis is based on the observation that there are many buyers and many sellers in the market who have similar information. Famed investment banker Jacob Schiff, managing partner at Kuhn, Loeb & Company for many years and called the Jewish Grand Duke of American finance (see Larry Haeg, *Harriman vs. Hill: Wall Street's Great Railroad War*, 2013) was said to have answered the question about how to make money in the stock market. He allegedly stated in his heavily German/Yiddish accent, "Buy 'sheep' and sell 'deer.'" To which his arch rival J. Pierpont Morgan was said to have remarked something along the lines, "If one could easily separate the 'sheep' from the 'deer', it would, indeed, make it hard to get rich." (As an aside, it should be noted that the "buy sheep and sell deer" advice has been attributed not only to Jacob Schiff but also Baron Rothschild, Bernard Baruch, and many others. No one seems to know the real source of the quote.)

Of course, Morgan was certainly not an EHM advocate (and neither was Schiff, for that matter). The idea had not even dawned on academic economists at the time (around the turn of the 20th century), and anyone suggesting such a thing to Morgan would probably have been called a "crank" at best or hauled off to a lunatic asylum at worst. What Schiff and Morgan both knew was that the stock market could turn on a dime, and sometimes for no apparent reason except for speculator "animal spirits," a term widely ascribed to Lord Keynes as we shall soon see.

During their fight for control of the Northern Pacific Railway, Morgan and Schiff witnessed the following: "May 9, 1901 was the stock market equivalent of a bungee-cord jump off the Brooklyn Bridge: perhaps the swiftest, most precipitous decline, then or since, in American stock values, and then the fastest recovery." (Haeg, p. xii). Now just what sort of "efficient" market could behave in this manner? What kind of "special event" occurring on the morning of May 9, 1901 could cause such a collapse, and what sort of reversal "news" could result in such a rebound? Surely the takeover of one railroad among the literally hundreds that existed in the United States at the time couldn't have inspired such a disturbance? In fact, there was no explanation other than irrational inefficiency.

Schiff and Morgan would have argued that perhaps the most important key to "beating the market" successfully was having more and better information than others. Put another way, every capitalist wants to be a monopolist, and a monopoly on information is the best kind. The EMH was advanced six decades after the fight over the Northern Pacific, but some of the lessons of that struggle are brilliantly brought to light in the Haeg book. Although this is not the place to rehearse that episode in American financial history, it is clear from the biographical records of both James J. Hill and Edward H. Harriman that they knew an incredible amount about the details of running a railroad. Unlike some of the speculators of their day (the names of Jay Gould, Jim Fisk, *et al.* might come to mind in the

discussion), these men spent most of their waking
hours getting to understand the economic value of the
properties they controlled or wished to control. Not
only did they read the financial statements of their
operating entities, they spent immense amounts of time
examining the physical properties under their jurisdic-
tion. Hill was said to have known costs down to the
penny and could figure out where traffic moves were
headed and what roads should be combined to get the
best east/west utilization of equipment. It was this sort
of information (and not rumors passed along on Wall
Street) that was used to find the "sheep" to buy and the
"deer" to sell. Both men were also very frugal both in
their personal lives and with stockholders' money.
"Even when Hill's position and wealth dictated he
should have a private [railway] car it was nothing fancy;
rather than give it some grand name he merely had it
stenciled 'A-1'" (Haeg, p. 26). A newspaper once
called him a "calculating machine" that "never permits
an invested nickel to be diverted from its duty of
making more nickels" (Haeg, p. 26).

Now it is true that financial markets were not regu-
lated then as they are today, and they were much less
fluid, but jumping from such facts to conclude that one
cannot compare 1900 with, say, 1960 is not entirely
convincing. In its very essence, the EHM states that, if
any one stock is "worth" more than the price for which
it is currently selling, buyers would enter the market
until its price rose to the point at which it was no
longer a bargain. Similarly, if a stock is trading for more

than its intrinsic value, sellers would drive the price down until it was no longer overpriced. This logic of market "equilibrium" is basically a tautology, of course, and it ignores the fact that some buyers may know a lot more than some sellers, and vice versa. Practitioners have known this for years and it is the reason most practitioners have rejected the EMH since it was first proposed.

Academic opponents of the EMH maintained that, in the first place, if the EMH were correct, it would be hard for professionals to justify the salaries that they are paid to find better-than-average performers. Second, many analysts have pointed out that their very presence is required for the EMH to work. "If they could not find undervalued stocks, they would not come to their desks each day; and if they did not appear, there would no longer be that vast army of competitors to make the stock market efficient and competitive! Moreover, many analysts point out that there are substantial differences of opinion over the same information. Thus, although every investor has available similar information, some see favorable signs where others find unfavorable ones. Furthermore, various analysts can do different things with the same data. Some may be able to forecast future earnings, for example, far more accurately than others simply because they employ a better analytical and more systematic approach. It is these differences of opinion and analytical abilities that make a horse race, and most practitioners...believe this is what the market is all about." (Thompson, Williams and Findlay, 2003, p. 5) In a very theoretical article, Grossman and Stiglitz (1980) argue as much as the title of the article suggests: "On the Impossibility of Informationally Efficient Markets".

Business historians have argued for decades that the long-term record of the stock market is neither competitive nor efficient. These inefficiency observers believe that people are motivated in the main by their emotions. To them, bull and bear markets simply reflect the optimism or pessimism at the current time. Returning to the Northern Pacific saga, John Graver Johnson, the esteemed corporate attorney who ultimately argued for Hill and Morgan before the U.S. Supreme Court, stated, "Important affairs are controlled far more by sentimentalities and personal feeling, than we are willing to admit" (Haeg, p. xii). Most of us have been tempted by the thought that economics plays a slight role in the financial markets and that investor psychology may in fact be more important. Indeed, there is good historical reason for one to feel that people are anything but rational when it comes to investing.

Several decades before the Harriman–Hill fight over the Northern Pacific, a very insightful book by Charles Mackay was published. In his *Memoirs of Extraordinary Popular Delusions and the Madness of Crowds*, he points out (1841, pp. vii–viii):

"In reading the history of nations, we find that, like individuals, they have their whims and their peculiarities; their seasons of excitement and recklessness, when they care not what they do. We find that whole communities suddenly fix their minds upon one object, and go mad in its pursuit; that millions of people become simultaneously impressed with one delusion, and run after it, till their attention is caught by some new folly more captivating than the first. We see one nation suddenly seized, from its highest to its lowest members, with a fierce desire of military glory; another as suddenly becoming crazed upon a religious scruple; and neither of them recovering its senses until it has shed rivers of blood and sowed a harvest of groans and tears, to be reaped by its posterity.... Money, again, has often been a cause of the delusion of multitudes. Sober nations have all at once become desperate gamblers, and risked almost their existence upon the turn of a piece of paper."

The history outlined by Mackay portrays a number of remarkable financial events from the past (1841, pp. 1–92). Among them was John Law's Mississippi scheme, which sold shares to gullible Frenchmen in a company that was to have a trading monopoly in a province of French Louisiana called Mississippi. Shares in the Mississippi scheme were eagerly purchased by speculators who knew that this "growth stock" would surely make them wealthy. In the late 18th century, it was commonly accepted that Louisiana was a cornucopia of precious metals.[1] Based on this

---

[1] They were correct in the long run. Two hundred fifty years later Louisiana was one of the oil centers of the world!

banality alone, people were willing to bet their fortunes on an "investment" in a company hardly known to them and in a location so far away that most Frenchmen couldn't find it on a map if set before them.

Next, there was the South Sea Bubble which enticed Englishmen to bet on a potential trading monopoly in the South Atlantic. Now this area was controlled by Spain, at the time a staunch enemy of England's. Even then it should have been clear to anyone in England with a farthing to invest that Spain had no intention of allowing the English into the area for commercial endeavors. Given this generally acknowledged political fact, however, Englishmen couldn't wait to invest their money in the deal. Believe it or not one such investor was Sir Isaac Newton who by 1720 was a very famous scientist and a rich man. In an "opinion" piece in the *Wall Street Journal* (July 2, 2018, p. A13), Andy Kessler briefly examines this history in the context of the most recent speculative bubbles. The title of his piece ("Look Out, Bitcoin has Lost its Tether") is self-explanatory.

The fevers induced by the South Sea speculation were replicated in other "bubbles." One of the more suspicious propositions was to buy shares in a company planning to build cannons capable of discharging square and round balls which were "guaranteed to revolutionize the art of war." Yet another offered investors the "opportunity" to buy into "a company for carrying on an undertaking of great advantage, but nobody to know what it is" (1841, p. 53). Blind pools of this sort became very popular even centuries later. The main objective of these pools, of course, was to separate the suckers from their money. Or, to once again bring the animal kingdom into the metaphor, "to shear the sheep of their wool as frequently as possible."

The Tulipomania, which visited 17th century Holland, provides yet another interesting story told by Mackay. It was commonly believed that every wealthy Dutchman wanted to have a magnificent garden of tulips. Many did and bulb prices began rising. Speculators saw this and bid prices up even further. Eventually prices levitated so high that tulip bulbs became more "valuable" than precious metals. Many thought the bubble would surely burst. Instead, prices rose even more as speculators bought bulbs to sell at higher prices to other speculators who purchased to sell at even higher prices to yet other speculators. Of course, eventually prices did begin to fall and then collapsed completely as everyone tried to get out of their tulip holdings at once. The term "bigger fool theory" of investing was coined based on this history.

One might have suspected that the appearance of Mackay's book in 1841 would have caused "investors" to think twice before they made the sort of foolish commitments Mackay described. One would have been mistaken. At almost the very same time as the publication of *Memoirs of Extraordinary Popular Delusions and the Madness of Crowds*, Jay Gould and Jim Fisk were manipulating the share price of the Erie Railroad in the United States. After the U.S. Civil War (1861–1865), northern financial speculators took over major industrial and railroad properties located in the former Confederacy. Most of these properties (especially the railroads) were in complete ruins. Yet numerous companies raised capital to buy them cheaply in order to "build" railroads that had no chance of ever being profitable. With the success of the government-financed transcontinental railroad (Union Pacific/Central Pacific), plus indirect governmental financing through extensive land grants upon the passage of the Railroad Act of 1862, the idea was to raise money on the stock exchange, fool investors, and then give out formation causing the price of their firm's shares to rise. This practice was regularly followed by the directors of the Erie Railroad who sold their stock (along with newly issued "watered" shares) to the suckers who thought Erie would run on to even greater heights. Within months of the "good news" some catastrophe would happen (a bridge collapse or some such calamity). Upon this announcement of the "bad news," Erie shares would plummet. Meanwhile, the Erie directors would have sold their stock short, making millions of dollars on the negative events. (For those interested in reading more about such financial chicanery as exemplified by the Erie Railroad but widely employed by others as well, see Adams and Adams, *Chapters of Erie*, 1956. Although there is a lot of "muckraking" and exaggerating in this book, it remains a classic on the subject.)

Such shenanigans followed throughout the rest of the 19th century and into the decade of the 1920s.

After the First World War, the United States entered a recession that was followed by an incredible financial boom. As Frederick Lewis Allen wrote in *Only Yesterday* (1964), "...the abounding confidence engendered by Coolidge Prosperity... persuaded the four-thousand-dollar-a-year salesman that in some magical way he too might tomorrow be able to buy a fine house and all the good things of earth" (p. 227). The binge got seriously underway in 1924 with the Florida land boom, where gullible people who had not even seen the swampland being sold (or even been to Florida for that matter) purchased sight-unseen lots for more money than economically attractive property could be bought in New York, New Jersey, or any other of the places from whence the investor-suckers hailed. The binge continued into the late 1920s, as Stanford University History Professor David Kennedy tells us: "Theory has it that the bond and equity markets reflect and even anticipate the underlying realities of making and marketing goods and services, but by 1928 the American stock markets had slipped the bonds of surly reality. They catapulted into a phantasmagorical realm where the laws of rational economic behavior went unpromulgated and prices had no discernible relation to values. While business activity steadily subsided stock prices levitated giddily." (Kennedy, 2005)

As we know, the binge ended in October 1929, with the stock market crash. The Great Depression followed and lasted until the outbreak of the Second World War over a decade later. It has been argued along the lines of the "chicken and egg" analogy: Which came first, or more specifically, which caused which? Did the market crash cause the Depression, or did the declining business environment of the late 1920s cause the crash? The subject is beyond the scope of this book but it is addressed to some extent in John Kenneth Galbraith's *The Great Crash* (1954). One thing is clear: The speculations of the 1920s, along with unsound investing and banking practices, undoubtedly contributed to the crash.

It was with the background of these speculative binges that John Maynard Keynes wrote *The General Theory of Employment, Interest, and Money* (1936). This is perhaps one of the two or three most important books ever written about economics. In the main, it deals mostly with why depressions come to exist and what should be done to eliminate them. However, the role of speculation and the stock market assume an important secondary position. Keynes argued that much of man's endeavors (including the stock market) were not well explained by economic theory. He believed that "animal spirits" exercised greater influence on many economic decisions than solid reasoning. His view was based on an acute understanding of human nature and a lack of belief in the classical economic models that had developed since the time of Adam Smith. He argued, "... our existing knowledge does not provide a sufficient basis for a calculated mathematical expectation. In point of fact, all sorts of considerations enter into the market valuation which are in no way relevant to the prospective yield" (1936, p. 152). He put his views rather strongly when he said, "... the assumption of arithmetically equal probabilities based on a state of ignorance leads to absurdities" (1936, p. 152).

According to Keynes, the stock market is similar to a game of Snap, Old Maid, or Musical Chairs. It is not, as claimed by many neoclassical economists, a serious means of resource allocation. Keynes maintained (p. 156):

> "... [P]rofessional investment may be likened to those newspaper competitions in which the competitors have to pick out the six prettiest faces from a hundred photographs, the prize being awarded to the competitor whose choice most nearly corresponds to the average preferences of the competitors as a whole; so that each competitor has to pick, not those faces which he himself finds prettiest, but those which he thinks likeliest to catch the fancy of the other competitors, all of whom are looking at the problem from the same point of view. It is not a case of choosing those which, to the best of one's judgment, are really the prettiest, nor even those which average opinion genuinely thinks the prettiest. We have reached the third degree where we devote our intelligences to anticipating what average opinion expects the average opinion to be."

In the stock exchange, pretty girls are replaced by equities that one speculator believes will appeal to other speculators. Thus, (p. 154):

"A conventional valuation which is established as the outcome of the mass psychology of a large number of ignorant individuals is liable to change violently as the result of a sudden fluctuation of opinion due to factors which do not really make much difference to the prospective yield; since there will be no strong roots of conviction to hold it steady."

Most practitioners even today tend to agree (at least partially) with Keynes' arguments. They feel that the lessons of history reveal economic analysis to be an incomplete approach to making investment decisions. It is suggested that esoteric discussions of whether or not the stock market is efficient are meaningless because whim and fancy may be more important than yield calculations in setting the prices of securities. Stock prices move up or down depending on the mood of the public. Frenzy and unbridled optimism make for bull markets, and gloom and severe pessimism produce bear markets. The states of optimism and pessimism often have little basis in economic fact.

In 1967–1972, a restatement of Keynes' view was made in two books that were religiously read by nearly every Wall Street participant at the time. These volumes go so far as to call Keynes the "Master" and credit him with insights that are still quite applicable. George Goodman, in his pseudonymously (Adam Smith) written *The Money Game*, pokes a bit of fun at his own profession and suggests that we have not really come terribly far in making the investments business a rational activity. The sequel, entitled *Supermoney*, argues that the 1970 bust resulted from eager traders trying to find the new Xeroxes and Polaroids, which were the "high-tech" stocks of that era. Unfortunately, they all too often found National Student Marketing and Four Seasons Nursing Homes (which subsequently collapsed). The mistakes were not only made by foolish individuals trying to get rich quickly; many of the more prestigious American financial institutions participated in running the prices of these securities to totally unrealistic levels. By the 1974 crash, many stocks (see aforementioned discussion of Service Corporation International) had fallen well below their "intrinsic" values. The money chased the "Nifty Fifty" stocks during the lead-up to 1974, only to find they weren't so "nifty" after all. Meanwhile, a shrewd analysis of non-tech, not "nifty fifty" stocks produced some really great bargains. Some of the stocks are still traded today at prices several hundred fold higher than in 1974.

Since 1974, there have been many more run-ups, followed by crashes. October 1987 (Black Monday), the dot.com crash of 2000, and the 2008 collapse are among them and we shall take a look at the impact these had on the EMH in the chapters that follow.

Chapter 5

The Impact of Information and Regulation on Market Efficiency

---

All I know is what I read in the papers.

— Will Rogers

As we have acknowledged in earlier chapters, information is more widely available today than it was at the turn of the 20th century or when Keynes made his observations in the 1930s. Whether this makes markets completely efficient is another matter. We would argue that perhaps there are degrees of efficiency, and that present (21st century) markets may be more efficient than the rigged game that was played a hundred years ago. The advent of the computer has made it less difficult to engage in the task of interpreting large quantities of data. Although it is certainly not clear that we have entered the world of perfectly efficient capital markets, it is likely the very chaotic world that Keynes described has passed.

Lawrence Summers, former Treasury Secretary and Economic Advisor to President Obama and former President of Harvard University has argued, "the ultimate social functions [of efficient financial markets] are spreading risks, guiding the investment of scarce capital, and processing and disseminating the information [about the future] possessed by diverse traders... prices will always reflect fundamental values ... The logic of efficient markets is compelling" (Summers and Summers, 1989, p. 166).

This is disputed vigorously by Professor Paul Davidson (the "keeper of the Keynesian flame," according to Professor Alan Blinder of Princeton):

> "The logic of the efficient market theory is compelling only *if* one accepts the presumptions of classical theory that the future is known and not uncertain. For financial markets to be efficient under the Summers' vision, information about the future exists, and market participants must know, with certainty or at least via probabilistic statistical reliability, future revenues and profits what will be associated with the enterprises underlying the securities being traded in the financial markets. These presumed to be known future revenues associated with the enterprise's use of productive capital are captured in what Summers calls today's 'fundamentals.' If financial markets are so efficient, then how does one explain that the financial markets for mortgage backed

derivatives after operating supposedly efficiently for several years suddenly collapsed in 2007 and thereby brought about the financial market crisis of 2007–2008? As Alan Greenspan found out it is difficult to explain why there is a global financial crisis if markets are efficient, as classical Nobel Prize winning theories claim."

Our view is that markets are not so perfect that all opportunities for better-than-average returns are eliminated, and they are not so imperfect as to render impossible the task of making rational choices. Ironically, however, it is also the massive computational power which has enabled rapid calculations to contribute to systemic financial crashes and contagion of a scale sufficiently large to make short-term market cycles far more volatile than in the past.

The EMH rests on the assumption that all investors (except insiders) have similar information at their disposal. Moreover, the EMH is predicated on the notion that all data have been impounded into market prices and that the current price of a security reflects the same. Advocates of a more anti-EMH persuasion advise that information is neither perfectly nor equally available and investors may interpret information differently. Since information is clearly important as a foundational input for both pro- and anti-EMH views, we shall examine several major sources.

First, a lot of information is generated by companies that prepare reports for both private and public investors. These include general economic analyses of industry and specific corporate prospects. Standard & Poor's and Moody's both prepare substantial reference papers and online research which are updated regularly to include the most recent financial and detailed reports on thousands of individual corporations. Charts of price performance over time, a history of important financial statistics, and an analysis of the background and prospects for individual companies are updated regularly (about once every 3 months as new quarterly reports are published by companies) and are available from most stockbrokers and online.

Brokerage and investment banking firms also publish their own reports that analyze and evaluate individual companies and securities. These are normally provided to customers at no specific charge (the cost is actually included in commissions and other fees that are earned from their customers). Many firms maintain staffs of analysts who specialize in one or more industries. In addition to the reports catalogued above, there are many private investment letters that are distributed to paid subscribers. These letters often are expensive; some have been prepared for years and are widely respected. Value Line publishes ratings and reports on hundreds of stocks and ranks stocks in terms of quality, potential short-term and long-term price performance, and yield. Securities are appraised by Value Line analysts and are given normative market values.

Much of the data and most of the reports mentioned above are available to a large audience. Suppose a respected investment firm puts out a "buy" recommendation on a particular stock. That information would most likely be made available to most other participants in the market almost instantly and there would be a tendency for this recommendation to be fairly rapidly incorporated into the price of this stock, and it might advance accordingly. There are other kinds of information, however, that may not be easily gained or understood. Important data are not always available to the general public, and even when widely disseminated some information is not easily interpreted. Data in the latter category often appear in the financial press and require specialized knowledge for proper understanding.

Many of the articles that are found in such publications as *The Wall Street Journal, Barron's, Forbes, Investors' Business Daily*, and other such publications are detailed and provide insights for the valuation of a firm. Often, however, it is not easy to interpret an isolated piece of information that may be reported about a particular company. Consider the case of a firm reporting its most recent quarterly earnings. Suppose that the results are immediately carried online by *The Wall Street Journal* and that the reported earnings were up significantly from the previous quarter and from the same period (quarter) in the previous year. Suppose further that the firm's stock price barely moved on this. The question may be: Why didn't the stock go up? The report is bullish and the firm has done well. One possibility is that professionals who have been following the company very carefully for years had expected the firm to do even better. Another possibility is that the market had discounted the good news. The improvement was expected and the price of the stock had been previously bid up accordingly.

The data that go into independent analysis may include publicly available information, such as a corporation's financial and operating reports (10-K's, 10-Q's etc.), but these data may be uniquely interpreted. Also, the professionals may have access to certain inputs that are not generally known to the public. Well-paid securities analysts spend many hours each week talking to corporate officers and employees of the firms that they follow. This is not inside information, but the best analysts can often discern facts from evidence garnered that equals that possessed by management.

Another EMH-implicit assumption is the presence of large, well-behaved securities markets. A market exists whenever there is an exchange of goods, services, or other property. A perfectly competitive market is one where there are many buyers and sellers, no one of whom can influence price. Perfect information is available to all participants in the market, and a homogeneous commodity is traded. Also, free entry of sellers and buyers into the market is observed. A competitive market must be sufficiently large so that any buyer (seller) can purchase (sell) at the going price (that is, the price set through the interaction of all buyers and sellers together). The U.S. securities markets generally satisfy the size requirement since many hundreds of billions of dollars' worth of stocks and bonds are traded daily here. This does not mean that there is a good market for every stock or bond outstanding. If there is sufficient trading volume (numerous transactions) in a particular security, it may be possible for trades to take place at a price very near the most recent past transaction price. However, there are plenty of stocks (and many more bonds) that trade in very thin markets where the number of transactions is so small that one may have to bid well above the last price to buy or ask well under that price to sell. Such a market is neither perfect nor efficient. Whether or not a particular stock or bond is traded in a generally efficient market may depend on its "floating supply." A stock with only 10 million shares in the public hands that "turns over" only 10% annually (that is, one million) could hardly be deemed "efficient." Such a security may show rather substantial price volatility from one transaction to the next, and no one buyer (seller) could accumulate (sell) more than a few shares at any one time without affecting the price. The aforementioned stock would exchange an average of only a few thousand shares each trading day.

Most stocks that are traded on an organized exchange have some degree of market depth. Although the total dollar volume of securities transactions on exchanges is less than in the over-the-counter (OTC) market (i.e., unorganized markets), it is generally the case that the dollar volume per security is greater for listed securities; however, this will not always be true.

The government bond market is conducted OTC, and the dollar volume of specific government issues can be quite large. Furthermore, some stocks that are widely held and actively traded are not listed on any exchange. The large stock exchanges have listing requirements that are designed to guarantee market depth. The New York Stock Exchange, for example, requires that a firm have a minimum number of shares outstanding in the hands of a minimum number of record shareholders. Additionally, a stock which trades only infrequently would not usually be a candidate for listing.

Organized securities markets have existed for some time. Securities were trading as early as 1602 in Antwerp and an organized exchange existed in Amsterdam by 1611. Almost all major countries (including Communist China) have at least one major exchange now. In North America, the New York Stock Exchange (NYSE) and the Nasdaq are by far the most important exchanges. In Canada, the Toronto Stock Exchange lists most leading Canadian industrial securities and a large number of mining and oil and gas securities as well. Other exchanges in foreign markets are even more important. Many securities are traded on several exchanges. An advantage of multiple listing is that extra trading hours may be secured for a firm's stock. Some securities also trade in the "third market," which is the OTC market for stocks that are also listed on an exchange. Both dual listing and third-market trading tend to increase the depth of the market for a stock and hence contribute to greater market efficiency.

Any securities transaction that does not take place on an exchange is said to be an OTC trade. The OTC market consists of numerous brokers, traders, and dealers who "make a market" in bonds and shares and are ready to buy or sell to each other and the investing public. Business is conducted via computer or telephone, and there may be no formal signal to other investors when a transaction has taken place. On an exchange, there is a record of each transaction, and an investor can observe the last price at which the security was traded. He or she may call his broker or follow the market online and find out at what price a particular stock opened (its first price for the day) and obtain the current quotation. In the OTC market, there may be no information available about the most recent transaction, and one's broker can only secure bid and ask prices on a security. A bid price is the offering amount for the purchase of a security; an ask price is the amount to complete the transaction. A "spread" between the bid and ask prices often serves to compensate those who make a market in a security. Depending upon the depth of the market, spreads may vary from less than 1% or 2% to as large as 5%; however, with the advent of algorithmic trading, typical spreads have shrunk dramatically.

Transactions in the primary (new issue) market are OTC trades. The primary (new issue) market is the first sale or new issue market. All initial public offerings (IPOs) are new issues. After a bond or share is in the hands of the public, any trading in the security is said to take place in the secondary market. It is interesting to consider the "efficiency" of the IPO market in recent years. As Thompson, Williams and Findlay (2003, pp. 15–16) point out:

> "The primary (new issue) market has been quite popular in recent years for speculative investors. The reason for this popularity is the fantastic price movements experienced by many stocks after initial sale (IPOs). In the late 1990s, it was not unusual for newly public stocks to double or even quadruple in the first day of trading. Some 'high tech' stocks went up by a factor of ten or more within days or weeks of their IPO. It was no wonder that just the mention of a new issue was often enough to get investors clamoring for 'a piece of the action.' It is interesting to note that this is not a new phenomena, and nearly all bull (rising price) markets for decades (actually centuries) have featured startling performers that rose to unbelievable levels even though these were brand new (or, in any case, not very seasoned) companies. For a while in 1999 and early 2000, just about any company with 'dot com' or 'e' or 'i' in its name seemed to be able to go public and have the stock price sky-rocket within hours or, at most, days. Companies that never made money (and some that had never made a sale!) were accorded market capitalizations (number of shares outstanding times price per share) that often exceed those of old-line companies that have been in business for decades."

An interesting example of the IPO frenzy was a "tech" stock named Aether Systems which provided "wireless data services and software enabling people to use hand-held devices for mobile data communications and real-time transactions" (Aether Systems, Inc. Form 10-K for 1999, p. 2). Aether went public at $16 per share in October 1999. On March 9, 2000, the stock closed at $315! During the "tech crash" in April, 2000, the stock fell to $65. It rebounded in only a few weeks to well over $100, but subsequently fell to below $5. The firm ultimately sold all its "tech" assets and ventured into mortgage-backed securities in 2004 when they were a money machine. Guess how that turned out?

The stock market has changed a lot over the past few decades. Stocks used to be traded in "eighths" and "quarters" (1/8 dollar and 25 cents). For example, the price of a stock might have been quoted at "10½ bid, 10⅝ asked." This meant bidders were willing to pay $10.50 per share and sellers wished to receive $10.625 per share. The resulting spread of $0.125 often went into the pocket of the brokers making the trade. Today, stocks are traded in pennies ($10.50 bid, $10.51 asked) so that spreads are much lower. The historical reason for stocks (originally U.S. Government Bonds before the advent of publicly held corporations) trading in eights was due to the division of the Spanish Dollar into eights (gold doubloons and pieces of eight). The British Pound was the unit of currency in the colonies, but the Spanish dollar circulated.

Additionally, decades ago the practice was to charge fixed commission rates per 100 shares of stock traded. This often meant that large quantities of shares (say 100,000 share orders) generated huge commissions for brokers. After "Mayday" (May 1, 1975), with the advent of negotiated commissions and substantial price competition, trades are often made at almost no spread and at commissions of less than a penny per share at discount brokers. This is a sign of a more efficient market.

One element that also may have contributed to the increased efficiency of the U.S. securities markets is regulation. Before 1933, there were no federal laws governing the operations of stock exchanges. Widespread manipulation and questionable practices were often observed. Although some states had adopted securities laws (called "blue sky" laws), in general, corporations were not required to and did not provide information to investors. Fraudulent statements (or no statements at all) were regularly issued by many companies. With the advent of the New Deal (the policies adopted by Franklin Roosevelt after his election as President of the United States in 1932), a number of laws were passed to prevent a recurrence of the events that led to the 1929 crash. Among these were major reforms of the securities business. For example, the Securities Act of 1933 was passed early on in the Roosevelt administration. It required full and complete disclosure of all important information about a firm that plans to sell securities in interstate commerce. Issues of securities exceeding a minimum in dollar value, and all issues sold in more than one state, were required to be registered with an agency of the federal government. (That agency became the Securities and Exchange Commission, or SEC, under another act passed the next year.) A prospectus must be prepared by the issuing company and distributed to anyone who is solicited to buy the securities in question. The prospectus must include all pertinent facts about the company, such as recent financial reports, its current position, a statement about what will be done with the funds raised, and a history of the company. Details about the officers and directors of the company are also required. Accurate descriptions about the firm's objectives, its primary business activities, projected financial statements (including any assumptions made), foreseeable risks to the enterprise, and the offering price of the shares must be spelled out. In the case of a new bond or note issue, how interest and principal will be paid must also be outlined.

The Securities Exchange Act of 1934 created the SEC. The Act was designed to regulate the securities markets and institutional participants in the market, such as brokers and dealers. Stock and other exchanges were required to register with the SEC (although much of the supervision of individual exchanges was left up to the governing bodies of each exchange). The 1934 Act also regulates the governance of publicly held entities. Regulations require most publicly held companies to file numerous reports with the SEC. Included are Forms 10-K (a detailed annual filing),

10-Q (a somewhat less detailed quarterly filing), and 8-K (a filing required in the case of a special event or change in the firm's circumstances such as the resignation of a member of the company's board of directors). A "Proxy Statement" is also required indicating when and where the firm's annual meeting is to take place, information about the top management and directors of the company (including comprehensive compensation data), and voting directions for directorship positions, selection of auditors, and other matters that may be brought to the stockholders for their approval.

Prior to the New Deal reforms of the 1930s, investors could buy stock on less than 10% margin (e.g., investors only "put up" 10% of the cost of the shares and borrowed the rest). Substantial leveraged returns were earned so long as stock prices were advancing. When prices began to collapse in late 1929, however, many people were wiped out in a matter of days as "margin calls" were made. Adding to the problem, investors tended to build their margin positions as prices rose by buying more shares with the profits earned. Thus, one might have put $1,000 into stock worth $10,000 in January 1929. As prices advanced by 20%, say, in February, he or she might have used the $2,000 profit to buy another $20,000 worth of stock. The commitment was still the original $1,000, but the investor now owned $30,000 in stock. As prices rose further, he or she might have increased his or her position to, say, $50,000. The margin in the investor's account, however, remained at only $1,000 (or 2% of the value of the stock). Even a small decline in price (say 1%, or $500) would prompt a "margin call," and the investor would have to come up with another $500 in cash, typically by the next trading day. If the investor could not raise the $500, enough stock would be sold to cover that amount. Now suppose prices fell just a little more, say 2%. This decline would be enough to wipe out the investor's entire investment. Furthermore, if many investors were "playing the market" on margin at the same time, their collective selling might tend to drive the market down by even more than it would have gone down otherwise.

The 1929 crash caused many investors to be forced out of their stocks as prices fell. The process of liquidating shares as prices went below margin levels caused further price declines which resulted in more liquidations. As Thompson, Williams and Findlay observe (2003, p. 22), "The snowballing effects of this phenomenon produced the major crash of October 29, 1929 and contributed to the subsequent collapse of both the stock market and the American economy."

As a consequence of the problems associated with margin purchases, the Securities Exchange Act of 1934 provided the Board of Governors of the Federal Reserve System with the power to set margin requirements for various securities. Since 1934, margin requirements have been set as low as 40% but have also been as high as 100% (no borrowing permitted). The sobering experiences of 1929 resulted in a revulsion to margin purchases in subsequent years. Nevertheless, there are many young "techies" in the market today who have only read about 1929 and would, like their grandfathers and great-grandfathers, gamble while thinking, "they know better." This is evidenced by the popularity of trading futures and options with higher notional leverage, and the rise in retail foreign exchange (F/X) trading with leverage in the 90% range as pre-1934 levels. Thus, "Big Brother" (Uncle Sam) considers it his job (among thousands of other such assignments) to protect these people from themselves. In so doing, perhaps the economy in general is saved from the effects of hubristic people making bad decisions.

The Securities Exchange Act of 1934 also regulates "insider trading." The Act defines officers, directors, and holders of more than a certain percentage of the shares of a firm as "insiders." Such insiders are required to file a statement of their holdings and any changes in their holdings with the SEC. This is done on Form 4, which must be filed within days of any purchases or sales of a company's securities. Form 4 filings represent by far the largest proportion of all SEC filings, a full 35% of the over 11.25 million electronic filings from inception in 1993 until 2011, with Form 8-K following up a distant second with about 9%. Insiders are also required to file Form 144 with the SEC, indicating an intention to sell securities by the filer. Form 144 contains information about prior sales of the company's shares by the filer as well as a statement on how the shares being sold were acquired (market purchases, options exercised, stock grants, etc.). Profits made by insiders on shares held less than 6 months must also be reported and may be legally recovered by the firm.

Over the years, litigation has greatly expanded the concept of insider information. During the 1970s, in the Douglas Aircraft and Penn Central cases, brokers got inside information (of bad earnings and impending bankruptcy, respectively) and informed selected institutional investors before the general public. Lawsuits followed and the SEC took disciplinary actions against the brokerage houses involved. Suits against the institutions found that second- and even third-hand possessors of inside information may be classed as insiders. In the Equity Funding case, information which did not even originate from the company itself but rather from former employees was considered inside formation. It is more or less true today that insiders are deemed to be such more on the basis of the information they possess than the positions they hold with regard to the firm. This appears to be the position taken by the U.S. Attorney's Office for the Southern District of New York where much litigation (and criminal prosecution) is effected.

As an interesting aside, given the increasingly important role of government regulation, it was not illegal for U.S. Congressmen and Senators and their staff members to trade on not-publicly announced information about the progress of legislation until 2012. One Senator (well known for his bombastic defense of the "little man" from Wall Street and corporate greed) knew that legislation was going to be passed which would change patent law and harm the drug industry. This great defender of the public good (and a multimillionaire to boot due to his shrewd investment in a rich widow) sold all of his drug stocks *before* the public knew these facts. For an act that would have sent a corporate insider to prison, the Senator was not even subject to reprimand by his colleagues. Indeed, he was rewarded by being named to a very high Cabinet position by President Obama. Changes to this advantageous treatment of insider politicians (and their staff) have been made, but what this says about the EMH is problematic.

Investors need to have benchmarks to measure how their respective efforts compare with the "market" in general. Professional money managers are often paid by how much they can beat "the market." Perhaps the most widely known benchmark is the Dow Jones Industrial Average (DJIA). This stock price comparative is an arithmetic average that appears in *The Wall Street Journal* each day and on computer screens instantly during trading hours. The DJIA is calculated by taking the price of each of 30 (committee-selected) blue-chip stocks, adding them together, and dividing by a divisor. The original divisor initially was simply the number of stocks in the average (12). Because of the obvious biases of stock splits (a two-for-one split would tend to cause the price of a share to fall by one-half), the divisor was adjusted downward for each split. The divisor now is a little less than just about 0.147 (yes, it is actually a multiplier since it has been reduced to a number below 1 for many years).

For many investors, the DJIA is "the market." When an investor checks the market or asks his or her broker to ask what the market is doing, he or she most likely will get a response "down 105." The broker means that the DJIA is down 105 points. The DJIA is not really a good indicator of market performance, since only "blue-chip" stocks are included in the average. The numerous stocks that are not blue chips are not included. The DJIA has been criticized by many even as a measure of blue-chip performance. Since it simply adds the prices of all included stocks before applying the "divisor," a stock that sells for a higher price receives a larger weight in the measurement than a level-priced one (as discussed above). There is also selection bias as stocks are dropped from the DJIA and others added. For example, poorly performing General Electric (GE) was removed in June 2018 and replaced by Walgreens Boots Alliance (WBA). GE was one of the original 12 stocks included in the DJIA and appeared for 122 years. After the removal of GE, none of the original 12 stocks is included today.

Many investors follow the Standard & Poor's (S&P) Indices. S&P computes a number of indices including the S&P 500, S&P 100, and specialized indices for foreign and specific industries. These indices include both the price per share of each stock and the number of shares outstanding. These figures thus reflect the total market value of all the stocks in each index. The aggregate number is expressed as a percentage of the average value that existed during 1941–1943 in the case of the S&P 500, and the percentage is then divided by 10. The S&P Indices are better overall measures of stock market performance than the Dow because more securities are included. Furthermore, the statistical computation of the S&P indexes is superior to the Dow Jones method. Although there is no single perfect indicator of average performance (at least for measurement purposes), there is a high correlation between the price movements of all stocks. Thus, if most stocks are going up (or down), almost any measure will indicate this.

As a final EMH consideration, we might observe the IPO market. It has been quite popular in recent years for speculative investors. In spite of the 2012 bust in the price of Facebook common stock which appeared to have cooled this enthusiasm, those who held on for a year and longer have been rewarded handsomely. Recent offerings have reverted to the old popularity. Consider the case of Uber and Tesla Motors. Both were darlings of Wall Street and closely watched IPOs. Tesla Motors debuted on July 5, 2010 at $19.20 per share, and doubled to $34 in a year or so, and has since skyrocketed to the $350 level by summer 2018. After 8 years, it currently loses more than $5 per share. Uber, the crowd-coaching company, was one of the most waited-for IPOs in recent history. When it went public on May 13 at $45/share it raised some $8 billion (out of a hoped for $100 billion). Several derivative plays on this stock are popular. At the time of this writing, the stock price has been unchanged, even after the announced departure of its CEO one month after the IPO. We shall see what happens going forward, but until then, one can only speculate on its future performance.

The efficiency of a market for securities that have never traded before is an open question. Speculative price behavior in this market suggests that "irrational exuberance" (in the unforgettable words of former Federal Reserve Chairman Alan Greenspan) may play a major role, however. All of this becomes important since the measurement of "beating the market" depends on which market one is trying to beat. This will become evident as we examine the "proofs" and testing methods designed to validate the EMH in Chapter 6. (*Note*: What does one make of Facebook and market efficiency? It went public at $31.91 per share, collapsed to $19.30 on August 30, 2012. It then hit a high of $218.62 in July 2018, only to crash again to $170 at the end of that month and approximately where it sits today. Perhaps another major collapse is in the offing.) In a perfectly efficient market, all of these results should have been anticipated and gyrations in price would have been anticipated and not have happened. Only in a world of "uncertainty" (outcomes not defined and probabilities not assigned) could this happen. Most of us would call this the "real world."

Chapter 6

Tests of the EMH

Over-diversification acts as a poor protection
against lack of knowledge.

— G. M. Loeb

It will be recalled, that, even in a world of perfect certainty, prices of securities could be expected to change over time as long as the income (dividend) stream is not instantaneous and constant. Indeed, price change would be necessary in such a case to cause the expected return for each holding period to be obtained. In a world of less-than-perfect certainty, changes in expected income or the required rate of return (caused, in turn, by changes in the level of interest rates or the perceived risk of the issue) could also cause the prices of securities to change over time.

It may be argued, however, that only the availability of new information or better analysis of already available information should cause the expectations regarding income, risk, and interest rates to change and, thus, prices to change for these reasons. If it may be assumed that: (1) all relevant information is available to all market participants; (2) any new information is spread and assimilated immediately; and (3) vast numbers of market participants employ the most sophisticated analytical techniques, then the securities market may be viewed as a "fair game." In other words, the expected price of a security in period one given the information available in period zero (assuming all dividends or interest are reinvested) is equal to the price in period zero times one plus the expected rate of return. This hypothesis also implies that (1) the excess market value of a security or (2) the excess expected return to be earned by holding the security both have, given available information, an expected value of zero.

Finally, it will be noted that both expected stock prices, expected dividends, and the expected rate of return are conditioned by available information. To the extent new information or better analysis becomes available, expected prices, dividends and rates of return can alter, and the expected rate of price change over time can shift. Adding the assumption that the timing of the arrival of new information in the market is a random variable, we see that shifts in the expected-price-change line, as well as movement about it, can be treated as random events.

We shall now examine various efforts to prove or refute the efficient markets hypothesis. The earliest empirical work was produced by the "random walk" hypothesis researchers primarily to attack the "technical analysts" (see earlier discussion in Chapter 3). Technical analysts for many years contended that by analyzing only the past price movements of a security, it is possible to predict future price movements and thus make greater-than-normal profits. The distress of the random walk followers was best expressed by Professor Paul Cootner over 50 years ago (1964, p. 232):

> "If any substantial group of buyers thought prices were too low, their buying would force up the prices. The reverse would be true for sellers. Except for appreciation due to earnings retention, the conditional expectation of tomorrow's price, given today's price, is today's price.
>
> In such a world, the only price changes that would occur are those that result from new information. Since there is no reason to expect that information to be nonrandom in appearance, the period-to-period price changes of a stock should be random movements, statistically independent of one another."

The early random walk researchers, then, concerned themselves with demonstrating that successive price changes were statistically independent of each other, that various mechanical trading rules based upon price changes did not yield profits statistically superior to a simple "buy-and-hold" strategy, and that "price changes from transaction to transaction are independent, identically distributed random variables with finite variances" implying, by the central limit theorem, that for numerous transactions price changes will be normally distributed (see Fama, 1970, p. 399). The Cootner volume contains many of the earlier studies and the Fama article has an extensive bibliography, so one is not reproduced here. Selected references are included at the end of this book.

Later researchers refined certain parts of the basic random walk argument. In the first place, it is suggested that price changes do not follow a true random walk (with an expected value of zero), but rather a "submart-ingale" (with an expected value greater than zero). Thus, the theory can take long-run price trends into account and accept a very modest amount of serial cor-relation in successive price changes. In view of the gen-eral upward trend of prices over time, it was surprising to many observers that the statistical case against abso-lute independence of successive price changes was as weak as it was. The challenge to the technicians has become to demonstrate that their rules can earn greater-than-normal profits. It has also been contended that price changes are not normally distributed about an expected trend but rather belong to the broader family of stable Paretian distributions of which the normal is only a limiting case. The implication for our purposes is that the "fat-tailed" stable distributions have an infinite variance, such that the usual portfo-lio approach employing variance and covariance can-not be used if prices (and, thus, returns) are so distributed.

Although the weak tests of capital market efficiency dealt with the inability to make profitable predictions of future prices from past prices, a second form of testing (called the "semi-strong efficient market hypothesis") attempted to prove that prices reflect all available information. These tests sought to demonstrate that new information results in a rapid adjustment to a new "equilibrium" price that, by implication, is taken to demonstrate that the price at any time must reflect available information. Specifically, the tests have taken events such as announcements of stock splits, earnings, dividends, interest rate changes, and so on, and studied (1) how rapidly a price adjustment was made and (2) whether the price adjustment was an unbiased evaluation of the information.

Most semi-strong EMH studies fell into one of two categories. The first considers what happens to stock prices when an event occurs. The second examines whether stocks of particular (publicly known) characteristics "beat the market" over time. Events studies go back many years. MacKinlay (1997) tells us that perhaps the first study was performed by Professor James Dolley of the University of Texas in 1933. His work involved taking a sample of 95 stock splits from 1921 to 1931, and examining what happened to the post-split price.

Over the years, studies have become more sophisticated, but all of them have certain common characteristics. We describe these in Findlay and Williams (2000–2001, p. 191f) as follows:

> "An event study begins by picking an 'event' (usually an announcement, so that it can be dated) common

to enough firms to get a reasonably sized sample (e.g., firms which announced a dividend increase). The study then takes all recent or otherwise usable examples of the event (which tends to make the sample become the universe) and assembles them in 'event time' (the announcement in each case becomes Day 0, the day before becomes Day-1, etc.). The study then takes the frequency distribution of stock returns on Day 0 (or Day 0 and +1) and determines whether the mean of the return distribution is statistically significantly different from zero. If, for example, the event is 'good news' and the mean is positive at 5 percent or 1 percent significance levels, the test is said to support the EMH. Tests of this sort are generally regarded to provide the most unambiguous support for the EMH."

This all sounds perfectly reasonable but the conclusion that the aforementioned tests actually prove the validity of the EMH is not. All these tests measure is that "good news" ("bad news") events, may accompany upticks (downticks) in stock prices. No study examined the issue (on average no less in each case), whether the magnitude of the price movement bore any rational relation to the news. While a failure of such a test would reject the EMH, a non-failure provides little support. Second, what is a "good news" event beyond something to which the market reacts favorably? Hence, what is one testing beyond whether the market is consistent? Some might say that "good news" could be determined by theory.

Consider dividend increases: under the old "bird-in-the-hand" view, this is good news. Under the MM (1961) view, it is no news. Under the theory that a dividend increase signals fewer lucrative investment opportunities, it is bad news. In fact, the market tends to view dividend increases as "good news." In that the "bird-in-the-hand" view was not popular with EMH, so researchers came up with a story that dividend increases are "good news" not because dividends *per se* were of value but rather because they were signals of higher sustainable levels of earnings. Based upon this last story, dividend increases being "good news" events was deemed consistent with the EMH. Circumstances when the specific price reaction is negative or insignificant are still deemed consistent with the EMH by its advocates as examples of the MM view or lack of investment opportunities views, respectively. Hence, any price reaction would be deemed consistent with the EMH.

Interestingly, all of these tests are conducted with a strong prior belief in the EMH. Contrary results are explained away or ignored. The example with dividends was provided earlier. But how about earnings? Originally, it was thought increase in earnings would be sufficient to be "good news." However, this did not always produce the "right" results (i.e., significantly positive announcement stock returns). The next step was to define "good news" only as earnings above those a model would forecast, or, later, actual analysts' forecasts. This generally produced the "right" results, until recently. Many firms have had earnings well above forecasts and their stock price still did not move. The answer, of course: Their earnings did not exceed the forecasts by as much as the market was expecting (and it is hard to subpoena the market). A scientific hypothesis should, at least in principle, be refutable. This does not appear to be the case in "tests" of the EMH.

As discussed above, these tests depend on the *mean* price reaction to the announcement. The distributions are generally skewed, such that the median would be closer to zero (and more likely not to be statistically significantly different from it). Hence, the size of the reaction will differ among firms. Further, some (or many) will be of the opposite sign (e.g., price declines on "good news"). What sort of similar "event" is being tested that produces price reactions of differing magnitude and, in some cases, direction? Let us be specific. Based upon these tests, we can say that an unexpected earnings or dividend increase will tend to be accompanied by a price increase, although not always, and certainly not of a uniform magnitude. How far does that take us toward being able to say that all public information is impounded into the prices of all stocks all the time?

In traditional science, there was a conventional wisdom at any point in time. If a new theory came along, a test was proposed. The conventional view played the role of the null hypothesis and the challenger played the role of the alternative hypothesis. To win, not only did the alternative need to be superior, but so much so that its superiority could only occur by chance 1% or 5% of the time (which is where significance levels fit into hypothesis testing). The EMH advocates apparently felt that, prior to their arrival, there was no wisdom in finance (conventional or otherwise). Hence, they felt no obligation to run tests by the old rules. Sometimes they tested their views as the null hypothesis (e.g., "no news" events) such that the higher the significance levels, the greater the chance they would win. The impact would thus be that the result cannot reject the null of efficiency. On that test, one cannot disprove that markets are efficient. Of course, that is no proof that they are either.

Another element of the "old" testing methodology was that the null and alternative hypotheses would be examined as mutually exclusive and exhaustive when possible so that a critical experiment could provide an unambiguous result and rejection of the null would imply acceptance of the alternative. The EMH advocates do not play by these rules either. On those occasions when they subject their views to the risk of bearing the burden of the alternative hypothesis, they lighten the load by setting a "straw man" as the null. Consider the discussion of "good news" events. What is the null? That the market no longer reacts as it did? Does rejecting that (and thus accepting some continuity of reaction) really imply we have no choice but to accept the EMH?

Finally, not only do researchers selectively interpret their own results, but by the time the results are summarized in textbooks, law review articles, etc., all of the exceptions, reservations, and potential alternative interpretations have disappeared.

Consider "granddaddy" of events studies (assuming the very early Dolley study of 1933 was a long-lost ancestor). This study was conducted by Fama, Fisher, Jensen, and Roll (FFJR) and published in 1969. FFJR looked at monthly data for the 60 months around the effective date of 940 stock splits from January 1927 through December 1959. The first puzzle involves why this very famous study concerned itself with an event that almost the entire spectrum of academia in finance and economics would have deemed a non-event: stock splits. (The Dolley work in 1933 looked at the same phenomenon, but this was 36 years earlier and the real economic effect of splits was not so nearly well understood then.) Worse yet, they purported to find an effect! Next, we get to the hypothesis being tested. An issue that they explicitly did not investigate (Fama *et al.*, 1969, footnote 4) was: Just why do firms split their shares? The only story they cite, which is the only one we have ever heard, is a version of managerial belief in the optimal range of a price per share, a story often repeated in the brokerage folklore.

The stated purpose of the FFJR research was as follows:

> "More specifically, this study will attempt to examine evidence on two related questions: (1) is there normally some 'unusual' behavior in the rates of return on a split security in the months surrounding the split? And (2) if splits are associated with 'unusual'

behavior of security returns, to what extent can this
be accounted for by relationships between splits and
changes in other more fundamental variables" (FFJR
in Lorie and Brealey (1972, pp. 186–187)).

One searches in vain for a potentially falsifiable statement in this. There really is no formal hypothesis
testing framework set up at the beginning of the paper.
Indeed, given that we do not know what motivates
firms to split their shares in the first place, it would be
rather difficult to hypothesize a market reaction.
Unfortunately, this tendency to avoid a formal framework has persisted in most EMH studies.

Once the data are presented, interpretations are
provided:

"We suggest the following explanation for this
behavior of the average residuals. When a split is
announced or anticipated, the market interprets this
(and correctly so) as greatly improving the probability that dividends will soon be substantially increased.
If as Lintner suggests, firms are reluctant to reduce
dividends, then a split, which implies an increased
expected dividend, is a signal to the market that the
company's director are confident that future earnings will be sufficient to maintain dividend payments
at a higher level. If the market agrees with the judg-
ments of the directors, then it is possible that the
price increases in the months immediately preceding
a split are due to altering expectations concerning
the future earnings potential of the firm (and thus

of its shares) rather than to any intrinsic effects of the split itself" (FFJR in Lorie and Brealey (1972, pp. 197–201)).

By the time these studies are reinterpreted at the text-book level, suggested explanations have become results: "The authors conclude that, although splits do not themselves affect the aggregate value of the shares, they do convey information about the company's prospects." (Lorie and Brealey, 1972, p. 103) Or as Professor Sharpe says in his textbook: "Tests of market efficiency demonstrate that the U.S. securities markets are highly efficient, impounding relevant information about investment value into security prices quickly and accurately" (1999, p. 103).

The textbook interpretation notwithstanding, it must be remembered that all FFJR did was present data and tell a story. One story, however, does not necessarily preclude another. Consider first the basic FFJR story: Splits signal dividend increase which signals a maintainable earnings increase. This would have greater appeal if splits and dividends were signaled by different agents within the firm. In fact, both require the action of the board of directors. This, in turn, implies a theory of why firms split their shares: to signal an almost immediate dividend increase. This begs the question again of why firms do not avoid the expense of a split and simply accelerate the dividend announcement. It becomes entirely inoperative in the instance of a simultaneous split and dividend announcement (a very frequent occurrence). It would seem that a rather bizarre implied theory of motivation for splits underlies the FFJR story. The example of the FFJR study is just one of many events studies used to "prove" the EMH, when in fact no such proof has been offered at all. Due to space limitations, we cannot replicate a critique of other studies. Thompson, Williams and Findlay (2003) provide many more such examples.

Additional studies into the dawning of the 21st century continue the neoclassical line. Lo and MacKinlay (2008, pp. 6–7) sum it up as follows:

> "There is an old joke, widely told among economists, about an economist strolling down the street with a companion when they come upon a $100 bill lying on the ground. As the companion reaches down to pick it up, the economist says, 'Don't bother-if it were a real $100 bill, someone would have already picked it up.'"

This humorous example of economic logic gone awry strikes dangerously close to home for students of the Efficient Markets Hypothesis, one of the most important controversial and well-studied propositions in all the social sciences. It is disarmingly simple to state, has far-reaching consequences for academic pursuits and business practice, and yet it is surprisingly resilient to empirical proof or refutation. Even after three decades of research and literally thousands of journal articles, economists have not yet reached a consensus about whether markets — particularly financial markets — are efficient or not. If this is the best story chaired professors at major institutions can tell, what is a practitioner (or court) to do? At a minimum, a hearing is required to determine whether a given case covers the $X\%$ of the time the EMH holds (or the $1 - X\%$ it does not). Certainly no support is provided for presuming (as many researchers continue to do) that $X = 1$.

In a crude sense, it could be said that the weak tests indicated that one cannot become wealthy as a technician (forecasting price or return movements based on past behavior), and the semi-strong tests suggested that, by the time one reads some new information, it is too late to profit from it. The theory still allows a person possessing superior information or analytical techniques to expect a better-than-normal return. A third form of testing (called the "strong efficient market hypothesis") went all the way to asking if there can be any information not reflected in the price of a security such that anyone can expect above-average profits. During the 1920s, it was claimed that "any day is a good day to buy a good stock." If the strong form of the efficient capital market hypothesis held, then, "any day is as good as any other day to buy any stock (or bond, or mutual fund, and so on)."

The rationale for the strong tests rested in a combination of the semi-strong tests (information assimilated in a rapid and unbiased fashion) and the fact that a great many supposedly knowledgeable and trained people are engaged in the securities business. It is argued that with so many people and so much information, there should be few if any true "sleepers." Studies have indicated that corporate insiders may have superior information and thus higher expected returns. Other investors, however, have not been shown to produce consistently higher returns. In particular, numerous studies of mutual funds have shown that their average performance is, if anything, inferior to the market as a whole.

It also appears that, even for individual funds, past success is an unreliable guide to future performance. In sum, it has been shown that the investor could do better picking securities at random than with the average mutual fund. And, because mutual funds are viewed as possessing as much information, analytical skill, and diversification as any investor, their inability to outperform the market is taken as very compelling evidence in support of the strong form of the efficient markets hypothesis.

In order to justify the time and money spent on the study of investments, it is necessary to come to terms with the strong form of the efficient capital markets hypothesis. Indeed, if the consumer groups gain additional strength, it may soon be necessary to place on the dust jacket of all investments books "Caution: Studies have shown that contents provide no advantage over random selection." Nevertheless, it should be remembered that the strong form tests were based almost entirely on mutual fund performance. Some may question the use of these institutions as absolute proof that, if they cannot outperform the market, no one can. For several reasons, it may be argued that mutual funds are an unconvincing choice for a test of the strong form of the efficient capital markets hypothesis. The compensation scheme employed by most funds encourages suboptimal behavior. Small funds take excessive risks in order to gain a place at the top of the annual performance lists. This is done in order to gain new shareholders and the subsequent profits derived from percentage-of-assets management fees. Even while adjusting for risk (say, using the Sharpe ratio discussed in Chapter 9), many investors ignore this information. Next, large funds cannot acquire substantial amounts of any promising issue without influencing market price unless their position is accumulated over time. Moreover, when a fund has acquired a large holding of a thinly traded issue, the position cannot be liquidated easily without influencing price. Finally, even if large funds could find small companies whose stock evidenced very lucrative future potential, the shares of these firms would represent only a small percentage of a large fund's assets. Hence, the fund could not increase its return significantly even if it did find securities that significantly outperformed the market. Fifth, legal requirements may constrain open-ended (mutual) funds to hold overdiversified portfolios. As a practical matter, the typical fund will hold well over on hundred securities. Nevertheless, unleveraged Markowitz efficient portfolios frequently turn out to be composed of fewer than 20 stocks, and, as additional securities are added, the positions become riskier without improving returns. Thus, superfluous diversification can actually increase risk.

There are a number of legal and institutional arrangements that tend to undermine many of the assumptions required for a capital market theory in addition to those that produce market inefficiency. In particular, it appears unlikely that market portfolios are (or can be) maintained by a substantial part of the investment community. In the first place, we can observe that legal and institutional arrangements eliminate some securities from consideration, much less selection, by certain investors. Banks and savings associations, for example, are effectively prohibited from owning any stock (with a few insignificant exceptions). Banks, savings banks, and some other institutional investors are also effectively precluded from owning low-grade (Ba or lower) bonds. Thus, whole classes of securities do not appear in the investment universe for the affected institutions.

More pervasive still than the outright prohibitions of securities are the various limitations on holdings. Thus, although most life insurance companies may legally purchase stock, they may only do so to a very small extent (5–10% of total portfolio). The legally required "crude" diversification also applies to banks. Many of the above restrictions, and others, reflect a rather curious legal philosophy that completely ignores portfolio concepts. It is generally agreed that most financial institutions serve a public purpose that requires that they continue to exist and avoid insolvency. It is then contended that this goal is best served by requiring the institutions to have a low-risk portfolio (this assertion alone is questionable). Moreover, it is felt that a low-risk portfolio is composed of a large number of low-risk securities. Hence, some institutions are provided with a "legal list" of high-rated, low-risk securities from which their portfolios can be selected.

Others, especially trust departments, operate under the "prudent man rule" requiring them to exhibit the care a prudent man would in managing his or her own affairs. Unfortunately, the courts seem to feel that this philosophy represents prudence. Thus, the investment manager must be concerned not only that the portfolio succeed but also that no individual security fail lest he be sued. "Prudence" usually prevails. It is an unfortunate truism that no trustee has been successfully sued for portfolio dissipation because he invested in government bonds. It should be observed that recent court actions indicate that the prudent man rule may eventually be abandoned. However, the growing demand that funds be channeled to "socially desirable" investments (which can include mortgages, municipals, minority loans, pollution control equipment loans, or loans to whatever other powerful special interest group desires cheap money) is causing an entirely new set of constraints to arise to take its place.

Additionally, it may be observed that some institutional investors pursue suboptimal policies by choice and thus create continuing opportunities for individual investors who do not have such policies. Institutions are not motivated by the same goals as the individual entrepreneur seeking profit. Hence, the "invisible hand" cannot be counted on to clear the capital markets more than other markets. In order to demonstrate that they are working for investors, mutual fund managers try to maintain close to fully invested positions. Although short-run bearishness may develop from time to time, long-run periods of being completely liquid (holding only cash or Treasury bills) would invite large-scale share redemption. Because management fees are based on the fund size, there is a definite reluctance to follow any consistent strategy that would reduce the volume of the fund's assets (even though long-run performance might be significantly better). Individual investors are not constrained to be in effectively fully invested positions, and it would seem logical that one could outperform most funds simply by acting rationally. Thus, if an individual who has superior predictive insight foresaw bearish conditions, he could profit by maintaining a bearish position (being out of the market) until his opinion changed.

We would suggest that the risk–return measures used in most of the efficient market studies (and in capital market theory discussed below) are not necessarily the same measures as those used by investors in *ex ante* decision-making. These measures are essentially *ex post* approximations of what investors may (or may not) have expected. Furthermore, the usual risk–return measures are based on annual holding period returns and may in fact overstate the true risk borne by the investment portfolio with a longer holding period.

What can we conclude about the EMH research? Amazingly, there is still no consensus among financial economists. Despite the many advances in the statistical analysis, databases, and theoretical models surrounding the EMH, the main effect that the large number of empirical studies have had on this debate is to harden the resolve of the proponents on each side.

We end this chapter with one added observation. "Average" returns may in fact be better-than-average to the extent that institutional portfolio constraints cause superfluous diversification and suboptimal investment policies, the yield curve for the capital markets may tend to become steeper. Thus, when institutions are confined to purchasing an inordinate amount of low-yield low absolute risk securities, markets may develop in the range just above the constraint cutoff. Consider the yield differences on investment grade (BBB) and non-investment grade (BB) bonds for example. This will make it possible for individuals to get even greater returns at higher level of risk than they otherwise would be able to obtain. Thus, even though apparent average returns would accrue to investors (differing only according to risk class preference), these average returns would tend to be higher than those that would prevail if institutional investors were not constrained. This phenomenon would not be evidenced in the numerous efficient market studies because a constrained equilibrium could still be stable.

Chapter 7

Anomalies

Once you know the identity of an outlier,
its interpretation changes.

— Anonymous

Precedent and inertia impede change in any significant field, such as the legal system or academic financial economics. In the *Erika P. John vs. Halliburton*
fraud on the market case discussed earlier in the
Preface and Chapter 1, the District and U.S. Supreme
Courts acknowledged a growing field of anomalies
research which calls into question the EMH. In spite
of Halliburton's presentation of numerous studies
providing "overwhelming empirical evidence" which
"now suggest[s] that capital markets are not funda-
mentally efficient" (Fed. Sec. Reporter,[1] 2014),

---

[1] 189 L.Ed.2d 339, 82 USLW 4522, Fed. Sec. L. Rep. P 98,003,
88 Fed.R.Serv.3d 1472.

"scores" of "efficiency-denying anomalies" make market efficiency more contestable than ever (Langevoort, 2002). But in the end, the U.S. Supreme Court affirmed the EMH principles espoused in *Basic Inc. v. Levinson* (1988).

The Oxford English Dictionary defines anomalies as irregularities, departures from the common order, which in the context of capital markets is the random walk theory and EMH. Moreover, in this case, the academic community has already provided succinct definitions for us: "In capital markets, an anomaly is a deviation from the prediction of the efficient market hypothesis." (Kahn, 2011, p. 1). Additionally, Cohen, Lys and Zach (2011, p. 129) tell us that anomalies are "empirical results that seem to be inconsistent with maintained theories of asset-pricing behavior." By the time the EMH had been finally well articulated, a long list of anomalies began to be published.

The managed money industry is not discouraged by the precept that on average no investor can consistently outperform the overall market, nor do investors grow weary of seeking outperformance. Investors will even pay a manager up to 200 basis points per year plus performance fees in order to outperform, hoping for breakeven in exchange for not having to manage their own funds. In mid-2019, a Google search on the term "seeking alpha" resulted in 9,870,000 results. Alpha is an outperformance factor in Capital Asset Pricing Models (CAPMs) after accounting for known "risk" factors.

For example, in the classic single-factor CAPM, the single risk factor is overall market excess[2] return, and by the theory, there is no outperformance (that is, alpha is equal to zero). Practitioners, and non-believers in the EMH, in their search for alpha, would develop quantitative screens of the stock universe which, when properly formulated into hypothetical portfolios, would result in long-term outperformance.

The CAPM of Sharpe (1964), Lintner (1965), Mossin (1966) and Treynor (1999) was for at least a decade the flagship model in finance arising from the EMH. Even after innumerable attacks on its supposed veracity, the model and its variants have remained the "go-to" models in orthodox finance. It is both prescriptive and descriptive. It has changed to keep up with empirical assails, adding risk factors to the original single-factor CAPM, but the fundamental systematic "risk" factor is the market excess return itself. As Professor Stephen Ross stated early on, "the attractiveness of the CAPM is due to its potential testability" (Gruber and Ross, 1978).

The notion of a stock's "beta" is simply that the return (or risk) of a stock is related in proportion to the overall market return. That rate of proportionality is called "beta," and it calculates the systematic risk or return which cannot be diversified away. It is related to the volatility of a stock in relation to that of the market

---

[2] Excess return above the risk-free interest rate.

as whole. A beta of one means the stock is about as volatile as the market, so if the market changes by 1% in a day, the stock should also move by about 1% (up or down); if beta is 2, then the stock should move twice as much as the market. Ironically, today beta is also an alpha factor, and can be invested in using the *PowerShares* S&P 500 High Beta Portfolio (SPHB) exchange-traded fund (ETF). The original, single-factor CAPM then predicts that if capital markets are in equilibrium, then all stocks will obey this linear relationship for the overall market return in their beta, and one should not find any outperformance factor (coined "alpha" by Jensen (1969) and by the anomalists).

Stock mutual funds and exchange-traded funds attempt to meet a particular benchmark, such as the S&P 500 or Russell 1000/2000/3000. Hedge funds and many other mutual funds have as their mission to outperform a given benchmark. As such they are still "seeking alpha." It is a stylized fact of money management that very few funds outperform their benchmark, and most do not even attain it. Yet, each year, hundreds of billions of dollars flow into such funds. New "risk factors" are constantly being researched, and, when promising, are exploited to uncover alpha.

The view of Graham and Dodd in their seminal 1934 book that there are stocks which as "overpriced," "underpriced" and "correctly priced" is summarily rejected by the implications of the CAPM. Their approach has been dubbed "value investing" by their students and practitioners, whereby portfolios are formed in a strategy of selecting stocks trading below their "intrinsic value." These are indicated by their lower than average price-to-book value (P/B) or price-earnings (P/E) ratio. Graham and Dodd unquestionably fueled the unrelenting search for alpha by the active money and hedge fund managers, who unfortunately as a group have never been able to consistently outperform the market. This fact assuages EMH believers. There are some notable exceptions, such as Warren Buffet's Berkshire Hathaway common stock, or Jim Simons' Renaissance Technologies Fund, but these are outliers. In mathematics and science, a well-placed counterexample is sufficient to invalidate a theory. And in real-world testing of the CAPM/EMH, these counterexamples are call "anomalies" by the sceptics, and "supposed anomalies" by proponents.

The same year Eugene Fama framed the CAPM in terms of beta (Fama, 1968), Edward Altman (1968, 2000) published his system to predict individual company bankruptcy and bond default. Altman reintroduced accounting ratio analysis as a legitimate tool in security analysis. He applied a multiple discriminant statistical methodology to a set of financial and economic ratios in order to rank companies' likelihood of going out of business, which in turn would adversely affect its stock price. From an initial list of 22 variables, five are selected.[3] These five variables were not the individually most significant ones, but considered using his statistical technique, as a group they did the best job predicting corporate bankruptcy. His system, modified in 1977, has been continually validated as seen in follow-on papers and reports. His 1–2 year horizon prediction accuracy over three epochs (1969–1975, 1976–1995, and 1997–1999) exceeds 80%, well above chance. This prognosticative feature of his model should not exist under the EMH. Subsequent to his work, various ratios and indicators have comprised the bulk of the factor-based anomalies. In the anomalies literature, the Altman system is a member of the fundamental data anomalies family.

Around the time of Ross's 1978 proclamation of testability of the (single factor at that time) CAPM, Basu (1977) published his backtest based on the price/earnings (P/E) factor. Firms with lower P/E had higher sample returns, and firms with higher P/E exhibited lower mean return than would be expected if the market portfolio was efficient. The P/E factor was found to provide above-average market returns over his study period of 1957–1971, as it has in countless revalidations after. Moreover, investing in the highest

---

[3] These ratios are: (1) working capital/total assets (TA); (2) retained earnings/TA; (3) earnings before interest and taxes/TA; (4) market value equity/book value of total liabilities; and (5) sales/TA. By 2000, Altman had settled on a seven-variable model, resulting in a prediction accuracy of over 90%.

P/E stocks has continually been shown to underperform the market.

The typical factor-based backtest goes like this. From a universe of stocks (for example, the S&P 500 or Nasdaq), one ranks each stock by its factor value, such as price/book value. One then buckets the ranked stocks into groupings, typically deciles. In the S&P 500, this would be 10 groups of 50 stocks each. One then forms portfolios from the deciles; these portfolios are typically equal-weighted, but weights can also be assigned related to rank or by some other technique. The portfolios are held for a time (rebalancing periodically in some scenarios), and then at the horizon time, one calculates the theoretical return performance based on realized market prices. One then comparatively judges the efficacy of the factor.

Multiple factors can be combined in more complicated joint ranking schemes, but this is the gist of the technique. There are many variants of this approach but the idea is the same. If there is a significant difference between returns of the "best" versus the "worst" group of stocks, this is an indication that the factor is doing something (providing alpha).

To illustrate Basu's result, the second author of this book analyzed the last 12 months' P/E for all tradeable[4] U.S./Canadian stocks for the period 1985–2011. For annual holding periods, the difference

---

[4] Stocks with a minimum market capitalization and trading volume.

between the best (lowest) P/E and worst (highest) P/E deciles was over 6% compounded annually, with the best P/E decile returning a compound annual growth rate (CAGR) of 18%. Compare this with the 27-year annualized returns for the S&P 500 and Dow Jones Industrial Average equaling 4.6% and 6.1%, respectively (including dividends). Basu's P/E anomaly is still going strong.

It should be remarked here that the personal computer (PC) revolution was just about to begin; Unix had been released on the Digital Equipment Corporation's (DEC's) PDP-7 minicomputer. A few years later (c. 1980), PCs exploded on the tails of the mini-computer hardware and software technology, built on the MS-DOS and Apple's PARC operating systems. This revolution will bring advanced computational capability to anyone's desktop, enabling advanced engineering, mathematical and statistical techniques to be designed, coded, and tested in an incredibly short timeframe. It will be a field day for empirical work in computational finance.

Four years later, Banz (1981) and Reinganum (1981) reported a significant negative relationship between abnormal returns and the market value of common equity for samples of NYSE/AMEX firms. Market capitalization is the share price of a stock multiplied by the number of shares outstanding. For the period 1936–1975, low market capitalization firms had higher mean returns than would be expected if the market portfolio were efficient. This famous anomaly is known as the *size effect*, and its publication shocked the finance community. Reinganum also revisited the earnings yield phenomenon (which is just the reciprocal of the P/E ratio). The methodology is, for all stocks in the S&P 500 (or NYSE or NASDAQ, etc.), rank each stock's market capitalization from lowest to highest. Form 10 portfolios based on deciles of the rankings. It was found that over long periods of time the lower market capitalization decile portfolios outperform the higher deciles in terms of CAGR. The difference in annualized return between the highest and lowest decile portfolios can be substantial, on the order of five percentage points, which accumulates impressively over timeframes such as 20–30 years. This is money left on the table, and unexplained outperformance.

Stattman (1980) and Rosenberg, Reid and Lanstein (1985) published their seminal anomalous factor which found that the average stock return is positively related to the company's accounting book value to market capitalization ratio (book–market ratio, or B/P). Benjamin Graham was including this factor as a screener in his popular book, *The Intelligent Investor*, as early as 1973. O'Shaughnessy (2012) reports that this factor holds up over very long time horizons, although there are also long subperiods of time where the highest B/M (lowest P/B) securities had disappointing returns. Overall CAGR for the 1927–2009 time period is

11–12%, about equal to the market return. The fleeting nature of many published anomalies will be further discussed shortly.

In a similar vein as Altman, Joseph Piotroski (1984, 2000) developed an accounting ratio-based prediction scheme, except instead of forecasting corporate distress his was designed to find future "winners," everyman's grail. He showed a viable system to separate winners from losers using fundamental accounting data in a universe of high book–market (low P/B) stocks. His nine fundamental variables included four profitability measures, three leverage and liquidity factors, and operating efficiency. For the period 1976–1996, he documented an outperformance of 7.5% annually. With shorting, the overall annualized return is some 23% (more than double the S&P 500 over the same period). Like Altman's fundamental data anomaly, Piotroski's system is still being critically evaluated and found to be evergreen.

Bhandari (1988) wrote on high debt/equity (D/E) ratios for firms resulting in returns being positively related to the ratio of debt (non-common equity liabilities) to equity, controlling for the beta and firm size. His D/E factor, along with Basu's P/E, Banz's market capitalization (size), and the B/M anomaly brought into question the adequacy of the single beta factor to explain common stock returns.

The book–market factor, combined with Banz's size effect, and spotlighted with these other pathfinding anomalies, brought a small crisis to the single-factor

CAPM. Since the EMH could not abide potentially legitimate sources of alpha, Fama and French (1993) published the now-famous three-factor model which adds size and book value to the market return as "risk" factors purporting to explain 90% of the diversified portfolio's return while at the same time eliminating most known alpha factors. The three factors are overall market exposure, market capitalization, and P/B. The goal was to better explain market performance and thus eliminate alpha, and it worked early on.

The same year as Fama and French's three-factor model was published, Narasimham Jagadeesh and Sheridan Titman (1993, 2001) published their seminal revelation of the "momentum effect," where by buying the better performing stocks (over the past 3–12 months) and shorting the losers produce anomalous returns. The outperformance lasts for at least 1 year, but it dissipates within the subsequent year. Their results have been repeatedly validated, both by Jagadeesh and Titman (2001) and by many others. Momentum is an unmistakable alpha factor with a magnitude of some 3%. Their result gave academic gravitas to the momentum strategies and hinted that trend-based technical analysis might not be dead on arrival as the weak form EMH stipulates.

Mark Carhart, now Chief Investment Officer and founding partner of Kepos Capital, formerly with University of Chicago and University of Southern California, incorporated Jagadeesh and Titman's momentum factor to the Fama/French (FF) three-factor model (Carhart, 1997). His results were seminal, not only for further documenting and quantifying the momentum alpha factor, but for providing a substantial datapoint in the "Managed Money" debate. Hendricks, Patel and Zeckhauser were able to demonstrate in their "Hot Hands" article (Hendricks, Patel and Zeckhauser, 1993) persistence in mutual fund performance, but they did not provide a good explanation. Carhart demonstrates that this persistence is in fact due to the momentum effect, not necessarily good stock picking skills. After controlling for the four factors, trading costs and management fees, he finds "very little evidence of persistent skill in stock selection, and any remaining small persistence disappears after one year" (Rubinstein, 2006, p. 340). The effect is still significant since most models using the momentum factor continue to include them, and it is generally recognized as a factor to control for.

Even the accountants were getting in on the action. Starting with Sloan (1996), hundreds of academic papers have been written documenting that stocks of companies with low accruals outperform stocks of companies with high accruals if the stocks are held for a 1 year period. Accruals are estimates and allocations made by accountants to align revenues and costs in a specific period. They are accounting estimates of the unknown amounts that attempt to show what the impact of the delayed revenue or cost would be on current profits. Much of modern commerce is based on contractual relationships where the timing of cash payments does not match when the services are delivered and the amount of a payment or cost is not fully known when the contract is signed.

Sloan (1996) shows that accruals are less persistent than cash flows and that investors fixate on earnings failing to correctly distinguish between the different properties. In particular, they overestimate the lower persistence of accruals (cash flows) when forming future earnings expectations. Consequently, this leads to an "accrual anomaly" where firms with relatively high levels of accruals experience negative future abnormal stock returns that are concentrated around future earnings announcements. Sloan concludes that investors do not fully comprehend the greater subjectivity involved in the estimation of accruals, causing them to make flawed decisions.

Communication and information flows are also enhanced by the emergence of an invention publicly known as the "Internet" in 1991. Consequently, the speed and breadth of anomalies research accelerated as more and more patterns are uncovered in the fundamental databases. Over time practitioners and other non-EMH researchers kept mining alpha, and in response by 2014 we have the Fama/French five-factor model (2015). Added were the operating profitability and investment factors; interestingly, the authors observe that the value factor becomes redundant in this model.

Other well-known anomalies are documented, some in popular audience publications such as the Stock Trader's Almanac, including calendar (weekend effect, January effect), seasonal (some touting 80% repeatability), and political anomalies.

The EMH proponents must be gratified to note that the effects of the majority of anomalies fade after they are published. G. W. Schwert (2003) states it thusly:

> "Many of the well-known anomalies ... seem to have disappeared after the papers that highlighted them were published. At about the same time, practitioners began investment vehicles that implemented the strategies implied by the academic papers. The weekend and dividend yield effects also seem to have lost their predictive power after the papers that made them famous were published...anomalies are more apparent than real."

Indeed, McLean and Pontiff (2016) verify that following an anomaly's academic publication, there is greater trading activity in the anomaly portfolios and the anomaly profits decline.

The new anomalies include such phenomena as those based on closed-end funds, initial public offerings (IPOs), index inclusion, "Siamese twins" stocks, insider trading, share repurchase, long-term price reversals, equity issuance, etc. More and more research is occurring in this field. Hou, Xue and Zhang (2015) examined 73 prominent anomalies; Harvey, Liu and Zhu (2016) reevaluated 296 significant anomalies, reporting that more than 33% of them are false discoveries. Hou, Xue and Zhang (2018) produced a voluminous review of 452 anomalies; they concluded that most anomalies fail to replicate. But their replication methodology intentionally omitted the smallest 20% market capitalization stocks in the NYSE. They do find, however, that the value, momentum, investment, and profitability anomalies replicate well.

James O'Shaughnessy in his best-selling *What Works on Wall Street* (2012) performed extensive backtesting over at least 45 years (1965–2009) on dozens of potential factors, reporting on over 315 models in his book. His results for all stocks (no filtering) include a 45-year CAGR of 11.01%, which compares well with the overall long-term (93 years) stock market return of 10%. What is remarkable is the extent of consistent overperformance and underperformance when ranking strategies. The difference in upside performance is 11% (for microcap stocks with Book Value/Price and momentum filters), and the difference in the downside is 12.35% (for the largest small stocks with a multifactor value combination). His results have been consistently demonstrated for four editions, and are fastidiously assembled.

The cat and mouse game is based on discovering mispricings but keeping them quiet. Were such results to be published, it would be fair game for the academics to incorporate them into a new model with new "risk factors" which subsequently eliminates any alpha. The modern era in the theory of finance occurs as researchers begin to incorporate the anomalies into the classical models. This circle of life has been going on for more than 50 years, and continues today.

Chapter 8

The Capital Asset Pricing Model

Interestingly, professional economists appear to think
more highly of professional investors than do other
professional investors.

— William Sharpe

While financial economists were testing the EMH (as in
Chapter 6), the idea was proposed that the original
Markowitz (1952a) work on portfolio analysis could be
used as a foundation for an overall theory of how assets
are priced in the capital markets. During the 1960s,
Treynor (1961), Sharpe (1964), Lintner (1965), and
Mossin (1966) proposed economic models that pur-
ported to demonstrate how financial markets operate.
This early work became known as the Capital Asset
Pricing Model, or CAPM.

The essence of these models was simple enough.
It was suggested that yields on assets should be higher

for "risky" assets than for less "risky" ones. This had always been a cardinal principle of finance and books going back to the beginning of the 20th century argued as much. The problem, however, was how to measure risk and yields. For bonds, the yield calculation was easier since the contractual terms for a bond are spelled out in its indenture. Coupon dates, principal repayment, and conditions of default are there. However, over time, a company's risk position might change (for the better or worse) and the overall level of interest rates might go up or down. All of these possibilities are items of risk such that measuring them was difficult. For equities, the task is much harder. Future dividend payments (to infinity at least theoretically) and the future price of the common stock should be forecasted. This is a monumental task which adds in forecasting risk as well as the basic fundamental risk of holding the asset.

The CAPM models had their foundation with Markowitz since he had used expected return, variance, and covariance notions to build his theory of portfolio analysis. Since he was dealing with the future, the forecasting task for his theory was formidable. This problem was dispatched by the development of the EMH since past returns and risk calculations could be substituted for future ones. A bunch of assumptions were required to make all of this work, however, as Professor Fabozzi tells us (2008):

"The CAPM is an abstraction of the real world capital markets and, as such, is based on some assumptions.

These assumptions simplify matters a great deal, and some of them may even seem unrealistic. However, these assumptions make the CAPM more tractable from a mathematical standpoint. The CAPM assumptions are as follows:

Assumption 1:   Investors make investment decisions based on the expected return and variance of returns.

Assumption 2:   Investors are rational and risk averse.

Assumption 3:   Investors subscribe to the Markowitz method of portfolio diversification.

Assumption 4:   Investors all invest for the same period of time.

Assumption 5:   Investors have the same expectations about the expected return and variance of all assets.

Assumption 6:   There is a risk-free asset and investors can borrow and lend any amount at the risk-free rate.

Assumption 7:   Capital markets are completely competitive and frictionless."

Indeed, some of these assumptions "seem unrealistic." However, mathematical tractability trumps reality in modern financial economics as we have seen many times earlier in this book (and will continue to see in the remaining chapters). Whenever these unrealistic assumptions were challenged in the literature (see Findlay and Williams, 1980, 1986, 2000–2001, 2008–2009; Findlay, Williams and Thompson, 2003;

Thompson and Williams, 1999; Thompson, Williams and Findlay, 2003; Williams, 2011; Williams and Findlay, 1974), Professor Friedman's theory of positivism (1953) was invoked to save the day. Professors Williams and Dobelman have always been prepared to grant that the CAPM

> "makes sense intuitively in that the market probably does price risk in some sort of reasonable way. Even the older professors of the pre-1950s era believed Treasury bills carried the lowest risk (and hence, the lowest returns), while increasingly risky securities (longer term government bonds, large capitalization corporate bonds, large cap stocks, small cap stocks, etc.) should have higher ex ante yields. Building a 'theory' to prove this turned out to be much harder than intuition would have imagined, however" (Williams, 2011, p. 9).

As we have observed several times previously in this book, the distinction between risk and uncertainty has all but vanished from the mainstream finance literature. An uncertain world is not easily quantified (if quantifiable at all). Perhaps admitting such would have been preferable to what has developed instead. Professor Williams concludes the following statement elsewhere: "Together with the construction of the 'joint hypothesis' of market efficiency and equilibrium, this resulted in a generally accepted theory of financial markets where risk was made benign (i.e., a mildly perturbed certainty) in order to achieve analytical tractability and where the acceptance of the neoclassical economics became a test of faith. The reality of this theory was the building of a massive edifice built on a pile of assumptions, presumptions, and ignored evidence. The long term capital management (LTCM) collapse, ... the dot-com bubble, and the Enron bankruptcy were the outcome of this element of the increasing blindness. No justification was provided for erecting the massive equilibrium efficiency edifice, no less 'betting the farm' on the inferences derived" (Williams, 2011, p. 9).

Going a bit further and bringing us to the financial crisis of 2007–2008, Professor Paul Davidson tells us (2017, pp. 1–2):

"On November 4, 2008 at the dedication of a new building, Queen Elizabeth of Great Britain visited the London School of Economics (LSE). While there she was given a briefing by academics at the LSE on the origins and efforts of the global effects of the global financial crisis and its resulting turmoil in international financial markets. The Queen is responded to have asked 'why did nobody notice it developing?' The director of research at LSE told her. 'At every stage someone was relying on someone else and everyone thought the other was doing the right thing.'

How is it possible that the many intelligent investors, bankers, brokers, fund managers and other financial market participants thought they were doing the right thing, when it was clear from hindsight that financial market activity was creating a situation that ultimately caused global financial markets to collapse and result in the worst global economic performance since the Great Depression? Why did not any of the many Nobel Prize Laureates in Economics warn governments and the public of this forthcoming global economic storm?

The answer lies in the fact that, at least for more than four decades, the mainstream economic theory that had dominated academic teaching, Nobel Laureate research, mainstream professional economic journals and the thoughts of financial market professionals and journalists is not applicable to the economic systems in which we live. Nevertheless this dominant mainstream theory's teaching is the foundation of the economic reasoning of economic students who then become bankers, entrepreneurs, politicians, government regulators, central bankers, etc. This mainstream theory, however, is a fairy tale fable that has no descriptive relationship with the operations of our market oriented, money using capitalist economy. Consequently what was seen as a way of doing good in this fairy tale economy, caused destructive economic forces in the world in which we live."

Chapter 9

Beyond the CAPM

Wall Street is the only place that people ride in a Rolls
Royce to get advice from those who take the subway.
— Warren Buffet

By the 1990s, the "joint hypothesis" of efficiency (the
semi-strong efficient market hypothesis, EMH) and
equilibrium (CAPM) had gained traction as the "new"
theory of finance. Even then, however, the growing
anomalies literature discussed earlier in Chapter 7
created problems for the CAPM, and a consensus
began to form that a new model, the arbitrage pricing
model or APM, would replace it. More recently, the
CAPM has been pretty much discarded by practitioners
(even those with MBAs from the University of Chicago)
and questioned in the academic literature.

As it turns out, the APM never gained a following.
Realizing this dilemma, Fama and French (1992,
1996) took two major anomalies (small firm and price

to book value), and placed them into what they purport to be a new equilibrium model. The EMH testing has continued with short interval events studies which are not as sensitive to a benchmark at least for measuring statistical significance. Thus, the accepted theory still implied that a person without private information (or indeed, any analysis) who purchased stock can expect (in the expected value, or on average, sense) to pay the "right" price and should a price divergence occur, profitable arbitrage would quickly return to the "right" price.

The new theory became the "joint hypothesis" of the EMH and the CAPM. Unfortunately, the joint hypothesis was so full of holes that it was hard to accept. Thus, as the anomalies literature developed, the joint hypothesis advocates asserted that since a joint hypothesis was being tested one could not tell which one was failing. (Seldom was it observed that both could be). So the specific equilibrium model employed (the CAPM) was picked as the culprit. From this, we arrive at the point where the advocates maintain efficiency subject to an equilibrium model to be named later. In sum, the price adjusts to news to continue to offer the fair expected return, "with nobody to know what it is."[1]

For these discussions, capital markets are generally assumed to be "frictionless." This basically means that

---

[1] For those experiencing *deja vu*, this phrase was used in one of the promotions in the South Seas Bubble.

taxes and transactions costs are ignored (assumed away). If such a market is in equilibrium (i.e., all securities are traded at the "right" price) and a disturbance (e.g., news) occurs, the equilibrium can be restored immediately (e.g., the bid-asked shifts without even the requirement of transactions). Hence, efficiency is but one of many manifestations of equilibrium and there is but one hypothesis (that is, there is but one "right" price) and we are left with the very crude efficiency discussed above. In particular, no inferences may be drawn about the expected return reflected by the price either before or after the movement.

To repeat the point, a demonstration of equilibrium in frictionless markets may well be sufficient to support an inference of efficiency. Yet, the doorstep of equilibrium is exactly where the blame for the failures of the empirical tests of the "joint hypothesis" is placed. Perhaps, however, there is a theoretical justification (e.g., no arbitrage conditions) for the belief in the existence (the near religious terminology here is not accidental) of an equilibrium model, even though its form has not been identified. It should be noted that a simple demonstration of no arbitrage in a market does not confer the full benefits of the broader equilibrium. Consider derivatives. With the edifice in place, expansion of these markets (so long as they cover operating costs) is unambiguously good. With the right price being set in the underlying market, all of the required adjustment occurs in the price of the derivative, which is in zero net supply. Hence, markets are simply made correct at no risk to the real economy. Now remove the joint hypothesis and recall that the derivative pricing models do not care which price adjusts to arrive at the specified relationship. It now becomes possible for the derivative "tail" to wag the economy "dog" with unknown impacts on the real economy. Similar arguments apply to reducing trading costs and expanding hours of trading.

It is also the case that empirical demonstrations of crude efficiency (e.g., no windfalls from trading on news announcements) provide no inferences about equilibrium or much else. Naive economists have suggested that the EMH might have validity solely as a logical, normative model. In its pure form, it is solely an empirical model. Expanding it to include a normative "story" suggests that the conclusions follow from the assumptions but the assumptions simply do not comport with reality. The latter criticism would be deemed invalid under the rules of Professor Friedman's positivism. Hence, we conclude that EMH cannot even be addressed as a normative model, no less evaluated.

The neoclassical arbitrage and equilibrium building blocks go back to Friedman's (1953) book (the real source of all the mischief discussed in this book). Friedman maintained that "rational speculators" are always present, who buy low and sell high. Such speculators dominate the market until other transactions are unprofitable and driven out of existence.[2] Hence, rational speculation is stabilizing and drives divergent prices back to their equilibrium level. Friedman's notion of "positivism" also makes a reappearance. Since all models are abstractions from reality, he maintained that their validity should be judged by their predictions rather than their descriptive accuracy.

Arbitrage used to have a clear meaning: The simultaneous purchase and sale of the same commodity at different prices so as to earn an instantaneous profit with no investment and no risk. Without time, investment, or risk, arbitrage could be conducted on a massive scale, and even a sole market trader could eliminate the price discrepancy. A key feature of arbitrage (which made it riskless) was that the commodity bought constituted good delivery against the simultaneous sale.

In the 1958 Modigliani and Miller (MM) paper (see Chapter 2), purported to demonstrate that, absent taxes, the value of an income stream should not depend upon the number or types of claims upon it (e.g., the debt/equity ratio does not affect the value of the firm). As the reader will recall, MM's arbitrage proof assumed two identical firms, one of which borrowed and one

---

[2] In the more recent literature, these are the "informed traders" who, sooner or later (depending upon the model), overcome the antics of the "noise traders" and cause the price to converge. To maintain "tractability," most of these models assume the market to be disconnected from the rest of the economy.

which did not. Ignoring taxes and assuming that individuals and firms borrowed at the same rate, they considered the return from buying shares of the levered firm versus borrowing personally to buy shares of the debt-free firm. They argued that, unless the total values of the two firms were the same, an arbitrage profit could be earned. In equilibrium, no arbitrage profits should exist. Hence, they claimed they proved that corporate debt policy didn't affect the value of the firm. We reviewed most of the problems with the MM analysis, but the arbitrage feature continues to be employed even today and deserves additional comment.

In the first place, even assuming two identical firms (which, of course do not exist in the real world), delivery of shares of a debt-free firm subject to a margin loan will not cover a short sale of shares of a levered firm (and vice versa). MM have changed the original meaning of arbitrage to include simultaneous long and short positions in statistically "similar" investments which are expected to earn differential returns over time.[3] Both positive investment and time have been added back to the meaning of arbitrage. If the correlation between the positions is less than perfect, risk has been reintroduced. In sum, MM have so altered the dialog that now even *Wall Street* discusses "risk arbitrage," without even knowing the notion's underlying pitfalls.

---

[3] David Durand's (1959) suggestion to describe this instead as a "switch" was duly noted and subsequently ignored.

The positive investment "problem" with "arbitrage" proofs of this sort has, over the years, generally been met by another assumption: the perfect short sale mechanism. The latter assumes that proceeds from the short sale are available for investment by the seller. Hence, any security expected to underperform (even if the expected return were positive) could be profitably sold short when the proceeds were placed in an identical security of average performance. In real life, of course, the short sale mechanism is far from perfect and identical firms are hard to find. In a 1961 paper, MM returned to show that, absent taxes, dividend policy did not matter either. Using similar proofs and constructs, MM introduced a new concept to the finance literature, symmetric market rationality (SMR). This assumes not only that all market participants are Friedman's rational speculator but further that everyone knows or believes this (i.e., everyone in the stock market assumes everyone else is rational). In sum, not only do Bigger Fools not exist but also nobody believes they do. Hence, nobody would buy when the price is "too high" or on momentum, and bubbles cannot exist. As MM themselves admitted (1961, p. 428):

> "Symmetric market rationality cannot be deduced from individual rational behavior in the usual sense since that sense does not imply imputing rationality to others. It may, in fact, imply a choice behavior inconsistent with imputed rationality unless the individual actually believes the market to be

> symmetrically rational. For if an ordinarily rational investor had good reason to believe that other investors would not behave rationally, then it might well be rational for him to adopt a strategy he would otherwise have rejected as irrational."

This assumption has been adopted in CAPM models for over half a century. It is a basic premise in "transversality conditions" which in general do not admit behavior that would cause the models to blow up. If the choice is between preserving the models and depicting reality, the prevalent philosophy has been to protect the models. Treynor (1961), Sharpe (1964), Lintner (1965), and Mossin (1966) assumed all investors to be essentially the same. That is, investors were deemed to possess the same information, have access to the same securities, and be able to borrow or lend at the riskless rate of interest (more or less the shortest "T" bill rate).[4] It followed that everyone would perceive the same efficient investment opportunities (called the "efficient frontier") and wish to hold the same portfolio on it. They then demonstrated that, in equilibrium, the only portfolio everyone could hold would be a microcosm of the market (called the "market portfolio" and often proxied by a broad index such as the S&P 500). Further, the market portfolio would be at the point of tangency with the frontier of efficient opportunities

---

[4] Criticism of the realism of these assumptions was met once again with a citation to Friedman's (1953) essay on positivism.

and a ray emanating from the riskless rate of interest (say, the shortest Treasury bill maturity), creating a Capital Market Line (CML) which is the basis for the Sharpe Ratio (1966) of portfolio performance. Individual securities would be priced in terms of their non-diversifiable (also called systematic) risk and would lie on the Capital Asset Pricing Line (CAPL), which forms the basis for the Jensen (1969) and Treynor (1965) measures of performance.

The question for our purposes becomes how the conclusion that all the shares fall on the CAPL is enforced. If everybody is in all essential ways the same (often called the homogeneity assumption) and knows this, the result will be obtained. Otherwise, to enforce the result by "arbitrage," we not only need the perfect short sale mechanism but also the agreement that a long (short) position in an underpriced (overpriced) stock and a short (long) position in a portfolio with the same beta is, in fact, riskless.[5] Recognizing the non-systematic risk of the former, even advocates quickly talk about many such positions, each small, to invoke the Law of Large Numbers (similar to the tales told for option pricing models if share prices are allowed to have large jumps and discontinuities).

With "arbitrage" defined as simultaneous long and short holdings of "equivalent" positions, "equivalent"

---

[5] Although the single-factor CAPM has apparently been rejected in the academic literature, the remaining candidates are multiple factor models where these same conditions apply to multiple betas.

has come to be viewed in statistical terms (mean, variance, and correlation). If historical data exist, they are often employed (as in stocks' beta coefficients). If no data exist, subjective estimates of return distributions and correlations (e.g., as in Bayesian analysis) are made. Future events are assumed to be subject to probability distributions that, in turn, are assumed to be subject to estimation. More complex models provide distributions of distributions, and the real world has essentially been assumed to be one of risk where the forces of ignorance and darkness are overcome by the assumption of probability distributions. Nor has the language escaped debasement. For several decades now, in the academic literature, this world of probability distributions has been described as "uncertainty." In other words, what 50 years ago would have been called "risk" is now called "uncertainty." What Knight and Keynes called "uncertainty" (see Chapter 1) has vanished from the Brave New World of modern financial theory. Long-Term Capital Management (LTCM) provides an interesting example of the above. When, after only a couple of years of operation, almost all LTCM's equity was lost in August 1998, LTCM's managers blamed their troubles on a "six sigma" event. This would be six standard deviations from the mean of a (presumably) normal distribution, an event with a probability of occurrence of less than one in a billion (i.e., they made the "right" decisions but were "unlucky"). Were they really that unlucky, or are there more things than are dreamt of in their probability distributions (e.g., that 29-year

Treasurys do not constitute good delivery against a short position in 30-year Treasurys)?

Now recall the CML discussed above, which connects the riskless rate with a tangency to the efficient frontier. In equilibrium, this is the market portfolio. Also note that these are the only two points on the line. The slope is called the market price of risk and the vertical distance is called the equity premium. Previously, we were discussing equilibrium within the stock market. We are now considering an equilibrium which also encompasses the debt market (and, in particular, an alternative as close to riskless as is available in the real world).

This is a very elegant theory, even though virtually nobody (no less everybody) holds the portfolios it implies. By placing the historical excess returns of equity over debt (the empirical equity premium) in risk/return space, it is implied that it is expected (in both the ongoing and unbiased estimator sense) and a risk premium. By connecting it to the riskless rate with a line (CML), the risk premium is implied to be linear to risk over the entire continuum (i.e., the market price of risk).

Estimates of the equity premium are not small. Depending on the proxies and the period employed, they range from 600 to 900 basis points. Indeed, this has puzzled researchers (i.e., there is a field of research called "the equity premium puzzle") and the claim that it should be no more than 100 basis points (and possibly negative) was the basis for the Dow Jones at

30,000 or even 40,000 articles. (See, for example, Glassman and Hassett (1999) who argued, "Our calculations show that a perfectly reasonable level for the Dow would be 36,000 — tomorrow, not 10 or 20 years from now.") The latter justified the ever-higher prices paid by investors in the late 1990s. When interviewed by the press, the investors thought they were participating in a continuation of the 25% returns. The resulting "equilibrium" proved to be "temporary."

Further, all stocks are not equally risky. If this massive premium exists between stocks and debt, one might expect to see some sort of premium across stocks. Yet, for at least 30 years and using either return variance or beta, no compelling evidence has been found. As discussed above, Fama threw in the towel on these measures a decade ago, and Professor Haugen (1999) argued for an inverse relationship of risk and return across stocks! In sum, the market price of risk between debt and stock has eluded detection within the stock market itself.

Given the perfect integration of the one-period debt market and the infinite horizon stock market assumed by the CML, one may observe that it is still intellectually acceptable to treat the debt market itself as segmented by maturity (e.g., Bodie, Kane and Marcus, 1999). Indeed, all of the term structure theories except pure expectations assume some form of segmentation. These range from a complete segmentation (where each maturity level has its own suppliers and demanders, who will not move) to a situation where borrowers and lenders have a preferred habitat and require a premium to move in either direction, to liquidity preference (where lenders prefer short maturities, while borrowers prefer long). A rising yield curve could imply anything from expected interest rate increases (under pure expectations) to a term premium (under liquidity preference) to differing supply–demand conditions in the submarkets (under the others). Without further information, it would be rash to call it a risk premium for lending long. In sum, if the equity premium is compensation, it may not (all) be for risk.

If there is this much ambiguity interpreting a yield curve of treasury securities, the true puzzle would appear to be what the equity premium purports to be measuring. Assuming a treasury of the appropriate maturity to be as close to (nominal) riskless as we can get, consider a corresponding high-grade corporate bond. After adjusting for the differing options and the expected value of default loss, any remaining return differential to serve as a risk premium must be close to two orders of magnitude less than the equity premium.

One response might be that it is easier to estimate the ability to pay a finite, stated interest and principal than the cash flow to shareholders over an infinite horizon and thus a lower premium is appropriate. It is here that the battle is joined. Is it merely that the unbiased estimators are quite imprecise (a variance, or risk, issue, such that risk aversion would demand a premium) or that such estimations cannot be made (an expected value, or uncertainty, issue)? The observation that everyone appears to extrapolate the present and recent past is again met with appeals to positivism (e.g., the market behaves as though it forecasts and performs recursions). The observation that the experience of America in general, and especially since WWII, has been unusually good is the subject of research in the emerging markets literature.[6] In sum, the equity premium is only compensation at all if it is expected (i.e., demanded in the pricing as opposed to merely hoped for).

The traditional neoclassical defense of the equity premium as compensation for risk (rather than, say, windfall) requires more assumptions to get us to the "return generating process." Not only does the market behave as though it forecasts and computes unbiased prices, but these only change on new information. Hence, we have "nature" pulling balls from an urn to generate stock prices. "Price discovery" is the market fumbling about to see which ball was pulled today. If different balls appear, we infer Nature has switched urns which, under the theory, means new information has appeared. The persistence of the premium implies it is compensation for something, and the only thing which the theory allows to be compensated in equilibrium (where we are assumed to be) is risk. What could be more obvious?

---

[6]This literature basically asserts that stock markets which survive over time are likely to show higher returns on average than all markets which ever existed.

Very recently, a new position has been advanced by the neoclassicals which is not risk-based. After observing that the growth in share prices over the last 50 years exceeds that which can be explained by dividends or earnings growth, Fama and French (2002) conclude that much of the measured equity premium over that period was pure windfall. Indeed, they state, "Our main conclusion is that the average stock return over the last half century is a lot higher than expected" (p. 637). Of course, if the equity premium contains unanticipated windfalls, the market price of risk does not measure what it purports to.

How can a market in equilibrium produce 50 years of windfalls? We are told, "The high return for 1951–2000 seems to be the result of low expected future returns" (p. 658). In sum, we appear to have arrived at the Dow Jones 36,000 result with the Dow only at 10,000 at that time. Thus, the past price appreciation was the result of a market willing to accept ever lower future returns. Fama and French state, "We conclude that the large spread of capital gains for 1951 to 2000 over dividend and earnings growth is largely due to a decline in the expected stock return" (p. 651).[7] Would everyone who has been holding shares over the last 20–50 years, while consistently (yet unexpectedly) reducing his or her required return for doing so, please

---

[7] This would have the further effect of making the parameters of the (already unobservable) purported equilibrium risk–return relationship time varying.

raise a hand? Yet this *reductio ad absurdum* is the logical result of the unquestioned adherence to the neoclassical paradigm.[8]

It is now apparent that what to Keynes was a convention has become (at least in a positivist sense) truth or reality to neoclassical financial economists. The market valuation has become "uniquely correct." Although none of us individually may know why this is so, in the aggregate as the market we do know it. While all of us individually may "hold our breath when the market reopens" each day, given that only a few industries are impacted in the interim, there is no collective reason to do so.

Along the same lines, we would suggest that Keynes' critique of stock market excesses as developed in Chapter 12 of *The General Theory of Employment, Interest, and Money* (1936) has been essentially assumed away rather than addressed and disproved by modern financial theory. Consider the newspaper picture contest. Under the homogeneity assumptions, everyone has the same aesthetic and under SMR, they ascribe this to each other. Hence, everyone picks the same pictures

---

[8] The Fama and French paper also illustrates the confusion of states of the world we discussed above. "The behavior of dividends and earnings provides little evidence that rationally assessed (i.e., true) long run expected growth is high at the end of the sample period" (p. 646). Observe that an uncertain quantity (average post-2000 growth of dividends and earnings) is reduced to a world of risk ("rationally assessed") and then to certainty ("true") in a single sentence!

(e.g., the market portfolio) and the contest ends in a grand tie. Even if the prize covered postage, the game would probably fail for lack of interest. Indeed, invoking rational expectations (i.e., one name for the normative "story" used to explain the EMH), the contest (market) would have known this in advance and never run itself (we have apparently reached the limits of anthropomorphism). Unwittingly, modern writers have effectively adopted Keynes' casino analogy for the stock market, but with an interesting twist: Investors are assumed to be the house, playing against "Nature." In other words, the game is assumed to have a positive expected return (the house cut), known odds, and independent realizations over time (i.e., results of one spin of the wheel provide no information about where the ball will drop on the next spin). Indeed, investors have an even better deal since they have no overhead.

We have argued that the belief that we live in a near-certain world can lead to numerous errors and that this is the result of (1) substituting risk for uncertainty, (2) making the risk benign (i.e., a mildly perturbed certainty) in the name of analytical tractability and (3) making acceptance of the model a test of faith. The result is a massive edifice built on a pile of assumptions, presumptions, and ignored evidence.

Risk (no less uncertainty) is not an *ex post* concept. If a portfolio manager is prone to speculation, the appropriate response is to cut him off at the beginning, not adjust his performance at the end. In sum, if the models are correct, the world is one of risk and the correct measurement can and should be performed *ex ante*. All that is being measured *ex post* is "luck." In such a world, however, the portfolios should be broadly diversified and "performance" would relate to costs (e.g., management fees, transactions costs, and taxes). A world of uncertainty is messier.

Perhaps before we go forward, we should state what we think financial economic theory has to say. Initially, it assumes a trade-off of risk and return, generally in frictionless markets. Next, it posits an infinite time horizon where information equilibrium exists. The result is manifested by a stationary return generating process where expected excess returns (i.e., in excess of the riskless rate) are only reflected in a rational risk premium. All relevant information is impounded in asset prices (such that the only source of expected excess return is the risk premium). The result is an equilibrium pricing model (a role filled at various times by the CAPM, APM, etc.) co-joined with a notion about the efficiency of asset pricing markets (the EMH) which together are sometimes called the "joint hypothesis."

With the advent of daily data, the former does not require a benchmark and has been relatively non-controversial. It is the latter which, for at least 30 years, has given rise to the "anomalies" discussed in Chapter 7. This, in turn, gave rise to the "joint hypothesis" so that the empirical failures could be laid at the door of the model of equilibrium (i.e., the benchmark) rather than the EMH. It is interesting to note that Tobin, in a very obscure paper (1984), classified the two types of tests as reflecting two different types (or levels) of efficiency: Information arbitrage efficiency versus fundamental valuation efficiency. In this framework, evidence solely in support of the first could not be cited in support of the second. Yet this is being done when event study results are cited to support the EMH intertemporally. In the Tobin framework, the failure of direct tests of the last would, at best (e.g., where the CAPM is blamed), result in no support. Over time, it came to be assumed that stock prices evolved from a stationary, statistically idealized return generating process with a constant, positive mean (where *ex ante* equals *ex post*). Markets were deemed to be frictionless and some version of rational expectations held over an infinite horizon, prior to which models converged.

What more would be needed for equilibrium to have been assumed? Since the demise of the CAPM, financial economists reaped all the benefits of employing an equilibrium system without having to specify and defend such. Indeed, the above framework is increasingly implied to be part of the EMH. It is hard to judge just where financial theory comes down today regarding the EMH, but there are so many holes in the research that only the most dogmatic professors still accept what was commonly taken as absolute "truth" 30 years ago. On the other hand, since the edifice of what is presently accepted as the joint hypothesis (see above) depends on the EMH, it should be noted that empirical failures of the joint hypothesis which have been found repeatedly by skeptics are generally blamed on the pricing model and not the EMH. Neoclassical financial economists have purported to fit statistical (i.e., probabilistic) models to uncertainty. Campbell, Lo and MacKinlay (1997, Chapter 1, p. 3) state:

> "What distinguishes financial economics is the central role that uncertainty plays in both financial theory and its empirical implementation. The starting point for every financial model is the uncertainty facing investors, and the substance of every financial model involves the impact of uncertainty on the behavior of investors and, ultimately, on market prices...The random fluctuations that require the use of statistical theory to estimate and test financial models are intimately related to the uncertainty on which those models are based."

The word "risk" has typically then been employed to depict deviations from the expectation of the probability distributions, and the term "risk premium" has been used to describe the excess return demanded to hold assets with such deviations. The "premium" has been supposed to reflect the return in excess of that offered by a certainty (in an "uncertain" world) or demanded by a risk-neutral investor. Note that Campbell uses the word "uncertainty" in the citation above. As we shall see, the words "risk" and "uncertainty" have come to mean the same thing to modem financial economists.

From this point, the more mathematical arguments have often employed a state preference (e.g., Arrow and Debreu, 1954) approach which has simply assumed equilibrium. Campbell (2000, p. 1516) tells us:

> "For roughly the last 20 years, theoretical and empirical developments in asset pricing have taken place within a well-established paradigm. This paradigm emphasizes the structure placed on financial asset returns by the assumption that asset markets do not permit the presence of arbitrage opportunities — loosely, opportunities to make riskless profits on an arbitrarily large scale. In the absence of arbitrage opportunities, there exists a 'stochastic discount factor' that relates payoffs to market prices for all assets in the economy. This can be understood as an application of the Arrow–Debreu model of general equilibrium to financial markets. A state price exists for each state of nature at each date, and the market price of any financial asset is just the sum of its possible future payoffs, weighted by the appropriate state prices."

It is from this approach that the basic (or fundamental) equation of asset pricing under uncertainty has emerged. Since this result purports to obtain so long as a no arbitrage condition holds, it is often cited to justify an equilibrium "anchor" of fundamental value about which asset (e.g., stock) prices fluctuate.

Findlay and Williams (1986) maintained that financial economists have modeled the real world as though it were one of risk (i.e., amenable to depiction by probability distributions). These economists have then substituted the one word for the other to arrive at an "uncertain" world characterized by "true" probability distributions. General equilibrium economists have done essentially the same thing with all markets (goods, labor, capital, etc.), and this is has led them down a blind alley. As Mirowski (1990, p. 300) observes,

> "It is just at this point that economists tend to lose their way, so it is imperative to make it clear how all the strands of our narrative converge on just this point. Neoclassical microeconomics is predicated upon the metaphor and formalism of potential energy which is at the heart and soul of the Laplacean 'demon,' in physics."

Laplace (cited in Capek, 1961, p. 122) argues the following:

> "An intellect which at a given instant knew all the forces acting in nature, and the position of all things of which the world consists — supposing the said intellect were vast enough to subject these data to analysis — would embrace in the same formula the motions of the greatest bodies in the universe and those of the slightest atoms; nothing would be uncertain for it, and the future, like the past, would be present to its eyes."

Not surprisingly, financial economists have gone down the same blind alley. Instead of the Laplacean deterministic problem, the market (as demon) has been presented as the solution to a stochastic dynamic problem. Unfortunately, just as neoclassical microeconomics is really a static solution to a much more complicated (and never realistically addressed) dynamic problem, financial economics is also a static (certain) solution regardless of all the bells and whistles added to make it appear otherwise. Put another way, neoclassical "uncertainty" is a certain world to which relatively benign lotteries have been added in which capital market agents may or may not participate at their option (recall the riskless rate as the opportunity cost benchmark).

Mirowski tells us where this approach has gone in the hard sciences and relates that it is not a new phenomenon (1990, p. 301): "More advanced texts in physics acknowledge that the problem of extraction of seemingly stochastic behavior from apparently deterministic processes is much older than the present chaos craze, dating back to the work of Henri Poincare." In modern economics, since the probabilities were deemed to be "true," Poincare's admonition (that even minor measurement errors can lead to large forecasting errors) has been judged inapplicable. Any troublesome issues have hence been resolved by assumption or redefinition of terms. Kogan *et al.* (2006, p. 196) have pointed out that, "Most neoclassical asset pricing models rely on the assumption that market participants (traders) are rational in the sense that they behave in ways that are consistent with the objective probabilities of the states of the economy (e.g., Radner, 1972; Lucas, 1978).

In particular, they maximize expected utilities using the true probabilities of uncertain economic states." We observe that rationality has now been defined as behavior consistent with the true probabilities of uncertain states!

A major goal of a prior article (Findlay, Williams and Thompson, 2003) was to note that in frictionless markets, one could not obtain equilibrium without efficiency. That is, no capital market agent would be content to hold his endowment at a current price which reflected abnormal excess returns (i.e., with information not reflected in price). Thus, efficiency is a necessary condition (or implication) of equilibrium, not a joint hypothesis with it. Without the equilibrium model, the EMH has only the crude meanings ascribed to it above. Might this imply a relationship between equilibrium and the three states of the world outlined there? A world of certainty in equilibrium would appear to be virtually a tautology. Everything is known and determines the equilibrium assumption (which is operationally fairly similar to rational expectations) seem plausible. Recall that correct probability distributions of everything until the world ends are being assumed. It would seem an increasingly reasonable assumption that the recursions could be performed, the tatonnement commenced, etc., at least to a first approximation. The problem, of course, is that we do not know all (or even many) future events, no less all their possible outcomes, no less the outcomes' associated probabilities, no less such that these sum to one.

Chapter 10

Conclusions

If thou be wise, thou shalt be wise for thyself: but if
thou scornest, thou alone shalt bear it.

— Proverbs 9:12

We come to this point considering what effect this
Efficient Market Hypothesis (EMH) has had in shaping
the intellectual landscape of the finance world, indeed
not just finance, but in jurisprudence as well.

Fraud is an emotionally and forensically charged
word implying intent, motive, and guilt. We do not
believe that any of the original researchers who contributed to the development of the EMH and Capital Asset
Pricing Models (CAPMs) were intentionally foisting
a scam or hoax upon the world. Remarkably, it turns
out that the EMH/CAPM became a movement with
a growing number of adherents, most of whom have
a motive to keep dissenting conclusions out of
consideration, and will employ malicious criticism and

suppression of contrary research of honest scientists in order to advance the ideological agenda. This behavior borders on the "madness of crowds" phenomenon (Mackay, 1841). The thesis of this book is that these tactics and motivations in fact contain true elements of fraud.

In the first annual report of the Securities and Exchange Commission (SEC) for fiscal year ended June 30, 1935 (Securities and Exchange Commission, 1935), we find the main objectives of the Commission's activities are to require a fair and full disclosure of the material facts regarding securities offered for sale ... and to prevent fraud in the sale of securities. By 1960, its responsibilities were unchanged but included supervision, anti-fraud enforcement, surveillance of security markets, and regulation of public utility holding companies.

However, by 1980, the Commission had accreted its purview to include the "broader interests of society and the economy," now declaring that the ultimate purpose of the Federal securities laws is to ensure the confident, efficient, and fair securities markets. And in addition, Commissioner Schapiro stated in 1991 that another of its goals is to *preserve* efficiency of the markets. This is now in the stated SEC mission as well as protecting "main street" investors. Is it any wonder, when such a mission is assumed, that it repeatedly reminds the Congress that its resources are too limited?

Robert Haugen, the pathfinding financial economist and anti-EMH researcher, an early advocate of low-volatility investing, and a pioneer in quantitative investing, wrote "the Efficient Markets Paradigm is at the extreme end of a spectrum of possible states. As such, the burden of proof falls on its advocates. It is their burden to deflect the stones and arrows flung at the paradigm by the nonbelievers" (Haugen, 1999). In this article, he reports that during a conference in 1998, a giant in EMH research was delivering a paper[1] on market efficiency, and pointed to Haugen in the audience and called him a "criminal, saying that he believed that God knew the stock market was efficient."

Other than in the arcane field of flat Earth debate or climate change, it is remarkable that of all the sciences, civility, and open-mindedness do not characterize scholastic debate when it comes to the EMH. Although matters have improved somewhat in the last decade or two, writers who depart from the EMH orthodoxy are still castigated, cut off from publication in premier finance journals, denied or withheld promotion and tenure, and can find their integrity of scholarship impugned.

The EMH, by design and evolvement, is much like the "Death Star" in George Lucas' *Star Wars* movie: On the whole impenetrable and impossible to vanquish. We recall how that story ended. We also keep

---

[1] According to Haugen (1999, Chapter 7, Note 5), this happened at the UCLA Conference, "The Market Efficiency Debate: A Break from Tradition," April 16, 1998.

in mind the many combat references in finance vocabulary. The good news though for investors is that, while the markets may indeed be largely efficient, there will always be pockets of inefficiency which can be responsibly exploited by those stouthearted enough to look for them.

Bibliography

Adams, C. F. and Adams, H. (1956). *Chapters of Erie.* Ithaca, NY: Great Seal Books.

Allen, F. L. (1964). *Only Yesterday.* New York, NY: Harper & Row.

Altman, E. I. (1968). "Financial Ratios, Discriminant Analysis and the Prediction of Corporate Bankruptcy," *The Journal of Finance* 23(4), pp. 589–609.

Altman, E. I. (2000). "Predicting Financial Distress of Companies: Revisiting the Z-Score and Zeta Models," pp. 15–22. Retrieved on September 4, 2009 from http://pages.stern.nyu.edu/~ealtman/Zscores.pdf.

Arrow, K. J. and Debreu, G. (1954). "Existence of an Equilibrium for a Competitive Economy," *Econometrica* 22(3), pp. 265–290.

Bachalier, L. (1900). *Theorie de la Speculation.* Paris, France. [Translated by Boness, A. J. (1964). "Theory of Speculation," in Cootner, P. H. (Ed.), *The Random Character of Stock Market Prices.* Cambridge, MA: MIT Press, pp. 18–91.]

Ball, R. and Brown, P. (1968). "An Empirical Evaluation of Accounting Income Numbers," *Journal of Accounting Research* 6(2), pp. 159–178.

Banz, R. W. (1981). "The Relationship between Return and Market Value of Common Stocks," *Journal of Financial Economics* 9(1), pp. 3–18.

Basu, S. (1977). "Investment Performance of Common Stocks in Relation to Their Price Earnings Ratios: A Test of the Efficient Market Hypothesis," *The Journal of Finance* 32(3), pp. 663–682.

Bernoulli, D. (1954). "Exposition of a New Theory of the Measurement of Risk," *Econometrica* 22(1), pp. 23–36. [Translated by Summer, L. Originally published in 1738.]

Bernstein, P. L. (1996a). *Against the Gods: The Remarkable Story of Risk.* New York, NY: John Wiley & Sons.

Bernstein, P. L. (1996b). *Capital Ideas,* New York, NY: John Wiley & Sons.

Bernstein, P. L. (1997–1998). "How Long Can You Run and Where Are You Running," *Journal of Post Keynesian Economics* 20, pp. 183–189.

Bernstein, P. L. (1998). "Stock Market Risk in a Post Keynesian World," *Journal of Post Keynesian Economics* 21, pp. 15–24.

Bernstein, P. L. (1999). "Why the Efficient Market Offers Hope to Active Management," *Journal of Applied Corporate Finance* 12(2), pp. 129–136.

Bhandari, L. C. (1988). "Debt/Equity Ratio and Expected Common Stock Returns: Empirical Evidence," *The Journal of Finance* 43(2), pp. 507–528.

Bodie, Z., Kane, A. and Marcus, A. (1999). *Investment,* 4th Edition, New York, NY: Irwin/McGraw Hill.

Campbell, J. Y. (2000). "Asset Pricing at the Millennium," *The Journal of Finance* 55(4), pp. 1515–1567.

Campbell, J. Y., Lo, A. W. and MacKinlay, A. C. (1997). *The Econometrics of Financial Markets.* Princeton, NJ: Princeton University Press.

Capek, M. (1961). *The Philosophical Impacts of Contemporary Physics.* Princeton, NJ: Van Nostrand.

Carhart, M. M. (1997). "On Persistence in Mutual Fund Performance," *The Journal of Finance* 52(1), pp. 57–82.

Cohen, D., Lys, T. and Zach, T. (2011). "Net Stock Anomalies," in Zacks, L. (Ed.), *The Handbook of Equity Market Anomalies: Translating Market Inefficiencies into Effective Investment Strategies.* Hoboken, NJ: John Wiley & Sons.

Connolly, R. (1989). "An Examination of the Robustness of the Weekend Effect," *Journal of Financial and Quantitative Analysis* 24(2), pp. 133–169.

Cootner, P. (Ed.) (1964). *The Random Character of Stock Market Prices.* Cambridge, MA: MIT Press.

Davidson, P. (2007). *John Maynard Keynes: Great Thinkers in Economics.* New York, NY: Palgrave MacMillan.

Davidson, P. (2017). *Who's Afraid of John Maynard Keynes?* New York, NY: Palgrave Macmillan.

Davidson, P. (Ed.) (1993). *Can the Free Market Pick Winners: What Determines Investment.* New York, NY: Routledge.

Dewing, A.S. (1919). *Financial Policy of Corporations.* New York: Ronald Press Co.

Dewing, A.S. (1922). *Corporation Finance.* New York: Ronald Press Co.

Dolley, J. C. (1933). "Characteristics and Procedure of Common Stock Split-Ups," *Harvard Business Review* 11(3), pp. 316–326.

Durand, D. (1959). "The Cost of Capital, Corporation Finance and the Theory of Investment: Comment," *American Economic Review* 49(4), pp. 639–654.

Fabozzi, F. J. (Ed.) (2008). *Handbook of Finance: Volume I — Financial Instruments and Markets*. Hoboken, NJ: John Wiley & Sons.

Fama, E. F. (1965). "Random Walks in Stock Market Prices," *Financial Analysts Journal* 21(5), pp. 55–59.

Fama, E. F. (1968). "Risk, Return and Equilibrium: Some Clarifying Comments," *The Journal of Finance* 23, pp. 29–40.

Fama, E. F. (1970). "Efficient Capital Markets: A Review of Theory and Empirical Work," *The Journal of Finance* 25(2), pp. 383–417.

Fama, E. F. and French, K. R. (1992). "The Cross-Section of Expected Stock Returns," *The Journal of Finance* 47(2), pp. 427–466.

Fama, E. F., Fisher, L., Jensen, M. C., and Roll, R. (1969). "The Adjustment of Stock Prices to New Information," *International Economic Review* 10(1), pp. 1–21.

Fama, E. F. and French, K. R. (1993). "Common Risk Factors in the Returns on Stocks and Bonds," *Journal of Financial Economics* 33(1), pp. 3–56.

Fama, E. F. and French, K. R. (1996). "Multifactor Explanations of Asset Pricing Anomalies," *The Journal of Finance* 51(1), pp. 55–84.

Fama, E. F. and French, K. R. (2002). "The Equity Premium," *The Journal of Finance* 57(2), pp. 637–659.

Fama, E. F. and French, K. R. (2004). "The Capital Asset Pricing Model: Theory and Evidence," *Journal of Economic Perspectives* 18(3), pp. 25–46.

Fama, E. F. and French, K. R. (2006). "The Value Premium and the CAPM," *The Journal of Finance* 61(5), pp. 2163–2185.

Fama, E. F. and French, K. R. (2015). "A Five-Factor Asset Pricing Model," *Journal of Financial Economics* 116, pp. 1–22.

Fama, E. F. and Miller, M. (1972). *The Theory of Finance*. New York, NY: Holt, Rinehard and Winston.

Fernandez, P., Carelli, J. P. and Pizarro, A. O. (2016). "The Market Portfolio is NOT Efficient: Evidences, Consequences and Easy to Avoid Errors." Available at SSRN: http://ssrn.com/abstract=2741083.

Findlay, M. C. and Williams, E. E. (1970). *An Integrated Analysis for Managerial Finance*. Engle Wood Cliffs, NJ: Prentice-Hall.

Findlay, M. C. and Williams, E. E. (1980). "A Positivist Evaluation of the New Finance," *Financial Management* 9(2), pp. 7–18.

Findlay, M. C. and Williams, E. E. (1986). "Better Betas Didn't Help the Boat People," *Journal of Portfolio Management*, pp. 4–9.

Findlay, M. C. and Williams, E. E. (2000–2001). "A Fresh Look at the Efficient Market Hypothesis: How the Intellectual History of Finance Encouraged a Real 'Fraud on the Market,'" *Journal of Post Keynesian Economics* 23(2), pp. 181–199.

Findlay, M. C. and Williams, E. E. (2008–2009). "Financial Economics at 50: An Oxymoronic Tautology," *Journal of Post Keynesian Economics* 31(2), pp. 213–226.

Findlay, M. C., Williams, E. E. and Thompson, J. R. (2003). "Why We All Held Our Breath When the Market

Reopened," *Journal of Portfolio Management* 29(3), pp. 91–100.

French, K. and Roll, R. (1986). "Stock Market Variances: The Arrival of Information and the Reaction of Traders," *Journal of Financial Economics* 17(1), pp. 5–26.

Friedman, M. (1953). *Essays in Positive Economics.* Chicago, NY: University of Chicago Press.

Friedman, M. and Savage, L. (1948). "The Utility Analysis of Choices Involving Risk," *Journal of Political Economy* 56(4), pp. 279–304.

Galbraith, J. K. (1954). *The Great Crash.* Boston, MA: Houghton-Mifflin Co.

Gerstenberg, C.W. (1932). *Financial Organization and Management of Business.* New York: Prentice Hall.

Gibbons, M. and Hess, P. (1981). "Day of the Week Effects and Asset Returns," *Journal of Business* 54(4), pp. 579–596.

Glassman, J. and Hassett, K. (1999). "Stock Prices Are Still Far Too Low," *The Wall Street Journal,* March 17.

Gordon, R. A. and Howell, J. E. (1959). *Higher Education for Business.* New York, NY: Columbia University Press.

Graham, B. and Dodd, D. L. (1934). *Security Analysis* (1st ed.). New York: McGraw-Hill.

Graham, B. and Dodd, D. (2008). *Security Analysis,* 6th Edition. New York, NY: McGrawHill. [Originally published in 1934.]

Graham, B. and Zweig, J. (2003). *The Intelligent Investor.* New York, NY: HarperCollins.

Greenberg, R. B. and Wolfe, Z. (2017). "Does Halliburton II Allow Defendants to Prove a Lack of 'Correctiveness' to Defeat Class Certification?" *The Texas Journal of Business Law* 47(1), pp. 1–9.

Grossman, S. J. and Stiglitz, J. E. (1980). "On the Impossibility of Informationally Efficient Markets," *The American Economic Review* 70(3), pp. 393–408.

Gruber, M. J. and Ross, S. A. (1978). "The Current Status of the Capital Asset Pricing Model (CAPM)," *The Journal of Finance* 33(3), pp. 885–901.

Haeg, L. (2013). *Harriman vs. Hill: Wall Street's Great Railroad War*. Minneapolis, MN: University of Minnesota Press.

Halpern, P. (2000). *The Pursuit of Destiny*. Cambridge, MA: Perseus.

Harvey, C. R., Liu, Y. and Zhu, H. (2016). "...and the Cross-Section of Expected Returns," *Review of Financial Studies* 29(1), pp. 5–68.

Haugen, R. (1999). *The New Finance,* 2nd Edition. Upper Saddle River, NJ: Prentice Hall.

Hendricks, D., Patel, J. and Zeckhauser, R. (1993). "Hot Hands in Mutual Funds: Short-Run Persistence of Performance, 1974–88," *The Journal of Finance* 48, pp. 93–130.

Hou, K., Xue, C. and Zhang, L. (2015). "Digesting Anomalies: An Investment Approach," *Review of Financial Studies* 28, pp. 650–705.

Hou, K., Xue, C. and Zhang, L. (2018). "Replicating Anomalies," Fisher College of Business Working Paper No. 2017-03-010, 28th Annual Conference on Financial Economics and Accounting, Charles A. Dice Center Working Paper No. 2017-10, July.

Jagadeesh, N. and Titman, S. (1993). "Returns to Buying Winners and Selling Losers: Implications for

Stock Market Efficiency," *The Journal of Finance* 48, pp. 65–91.

Jagadeesh, N. and Titman, S. (2001). "Profitability of Momentum Strategies: An Evaluation of Alternative Explanations," *The Journal of Finance* 56(2), pp. 699–720.

Jensen, M. (1969). "Risk, the Pricing of Capital Assets, and the Evaluation of Investment Portfolio," *Journal of Business* 42(2), pp. 167–247.

Kahn, M. (2011). "Conceptual Foundations of Capital Market Anomalies," in Zacks, L. (Ed.), *The Handbook of Equity Market Anomalies: Translating Market Inefficiencies into Effective Investment Strategies.* Hoboken, NJ: John Wiley & Sons.

Kennedy, D. M. (2005). *Freedom from Fear: The American People in Depression and War.* New York, NY: Oxford University Press.

Kessler, A. (2 July 2018). "Look Out, Bitcoin has Lost its Tether", *The Wall Street Journal*, p. A13.

Keynes, J. M. (1921). *The Treatise on Probability.* London, UK: Macmillan.

Keynes, J. M. (1924). *A Tract on Monetary Reform.* Amherst, NY: Prometheus Books.

Keynes, J. M. (1936). *The General Theory of Employment, Interest, and Money.* London, UK: Macmillan.

Knight, F. (1921). *Risk, Uncertainty and Profit.* New York, NY: Harper and Row.

Kogan, L., *et al.* (2006). "The Price Impact and Survival of Irrational Traders," *The Journal of Finance* 61(1), pp. 195–229.

Lakonishok, L. and Maberly, E. (1990). "The Weekend Effect: Trading Patterns of Individual and

Institutional Investors," *The Journal of Finance* 45(1), pp. 231–243.

Langevoort, D. C. (2002). "Taming the Animal Spirits of the Stock Markets: A Behavioral Approach to Securities Regulation," *Northwestern University Law Review* 97(1).

Lintner, J. (1965). "The Valuation of Risk Assets and the Selection of Risky Investments in Stock Portfolios and Capital Budgets," *Review of Economics and Statistics* 47(1), pp. 13–37.

Lo, A. W. and MacKinlay, A. C. (1988). "Stock Market Prices Do Not Follow Random Walks: Evidence from a Simple Specification Test," *Review of Financial Studies* 1(1), pp. 41–66.

Lo, A. W. and MacKinlay, A. C. (2008). *A Non-Random Walk Down Wall Street.* Princeton, NJ: Princeton University Press.

Lorie, J. and Brealey, A. (eds.) (1972). *Modern Developments in Investment Management.* New York: Praeger Press.

Lucas, R. (1978). "Asset Prices in an Exchange Economy," *Econometrica* 46(6), pp. 1429–1445.

Maberly, E. (1995). "Eureka! Eureka! Discovery of the Monday Effect Belongs to the Ancient Scribes," *Financial Analysts Journal* 51(5), pp. 10–11.

Mackay, C. (2011). *Extraordinary Popular Delusions and the Madness of Crowds.* Cambridge, UK: Cambridge University Press (originally published 1841).

MacKinlay, A. C. (1997). "Event Studies in Economics and Finance," *Journal of Economic Literature* 35(1), pp. 13–39.

Malkiel, G. B. (2019). *A Random Walk Down Wall Street: The Time-tested Strategy for Successful Investing,*

12th Edition. New York, NY: W. W. Norton and Company.

Markowitz, H. (1952a). "Portfolio Selection," *The Journal of Finance* 7(1), pp. 77–91.

Markowitz, H. (1952b). "The Utility of Wealth," *Journal of Political Economy* 60, pp. 151–158.

Markowitz, H. (1956). "The Optimization of a Quadratic Function Subject to Linear Constraints," *Naval Research Logistics Quarterly* 3(1–2), pp. 111–133.

Markowitz, H. (1959). *Portfolio Selection*. New York, NY: John Wiley for the Cowles Foundation.

Mead, E.S. (1923). *Corporation Finance*. New York: D. Appleton and Co.

McLean, R. D. and Pontiff, J. (2016). "Does Academic Research Destroy Stock Return Predictability?" *The Journal of Finance* 71, pp. 5–31.

Miller, M. and Modigliani, F. (1961). "Dividend Policy, Growth, and the Valuation of Shares," *Journal of Business*, pp. 411–433.

Mirowski, P. (1990). "From Mandelbrot to Chaos in Economic Theory," *Southern Economic Journal* 57(2), pp. 289–307.

Modigliani, F. and Miller, M. (1958). "The Cost of Capital, Corporation Finance, and the Theory of Investment," *American Economic Review* 48(3), pp. 261–297.

Mossin, J. (1966). "Equilibrium in a Capital Asset Market," *Econometrica* 34(4), pp. 768–783.

O'Shaughnessy, J. (2012). *What Works on Wall Street*, 4th Edition. New York, NY: McGraw-Hill.

Pierson, F. C. (1959). *The Education of American Businessmen*. New York, NY: John Wiley.

Piotroski, J. D. (1984). "Value Investing: The Use of Historical Financial Statement Information to Separate Winners from Losers", Selected Paper 84, The University of Chicago Graduate School of Business.

Piotroski, J. D. (2000). "Value Investing: The Use of Historical Financial Statement Information to Separate Winners from Losers." *Journal of Accounting Research* 38, pp. 1–41.

Putnam, B. H., Norland, E. and Arasu, K. T. (2019). *Economics Gone Astray.* Hackensack, NJ: World Scientific.

Radner, R. (1972). "Existence of Equilibrium of Plans, Prices, and Price Expectations in a Sequence of Markets," *Econometrica* 40(2), pp. 289–303.

Reinganum, M. R. (1981). "Misspecification of Capital Asset Pricing: Empirical Anomalies Based on Earnings Yields and Market Values," *Journal of Financial Economics* 9, pp. 19–46.

Ripley, W.Z. (1915). *Railroads: Finance and Organization.* New York: Longmans, Green, and Co.

Roberts, H. (1959). "Stock-Market 'Patterns' and Financial Analysis: Methodological Suggestions," *The Journal of Finance* 14(1), pp. 1–10.

Roll, R. (2000). "Rational Infinitely — Lived Assets Must be Non-Stationary," UCLA Working Paper, November.

Rosenberg, B., Reid, K. and Lanstein, R. (1985). "Persuasive Evidence of Market Inefficiency," *Journal of Portfolio Management* 11(3), pp. 9–16.

Rubinstein, M. (2006). *A History of the Theory of Investment.* New York, NY: John Wiley & Sons.

Samuelson, P. A. (1967). "General Proof that Diversification Pays," *The Journal of Financial and Quantitative Analysis* 2(1), pp. 1–13.

Schwartz, V. E. and Appel, C. E. (2016). "Rebutting the Fraud on the Market Presumption in Securities Fraud Class Actions: Halliburton II Opens the Door," *Michigan Business & Entrepreneurial Law Review* 5(1).

Schwert, G. W. (2003). "Anomalies and Market Efficiency," in Constantinides, G. M., Harris, M. and Stulz, R. M. (Ed.), *Handbook of the Economics of Finance*, 1st Edition, Vol. 1, Chapter 15. North Holland, the Netherlands: Elsevier, pp. 939–974.

Securities and Exchange Commission (1935). *First Annual Report of the Securities and Exchange Commission for Fiscal Year Ended June 30, 1935*. Washington, DC: US Government Printing Office.

Shaffner, F. I. (1936). *The Problem of Investment*. New York, Wiley & Sons.

Sharpe, W. F. (1963). "A Simplified Model for Portfolio Analysis," *Management Science* 9(2), pp. 277–293.

Sharpe, W. F. (1964). "Capital Asset Prices: A Theory of Market Equilibrium under Conditions of Risk," *The Journal of Finance* 19(3), pp. 425–442.

Sharpe, W. F. (1966). "Mutual Fund Performance," *Journal of Business* 39(1), pp. 119–138.

Sharpe, W. F. (1972). "Risk, Market Sensitivity and Diversification," *Financial Analysis Journal* 28(1), pp. 74–79.

Sharpe, W. F., Alexander, G. J. and Bailey, J. V. (1999). *Investments*, 6th Edition. Upper Saddle River, NJ: Prentice-Hall.

Shiller, R. F. (2005). "Behavioral Economics and Institutional Innovation," *Southern Economic Journal* 72(2), pp. 269–283.

Siegel, J. J. (2009). "Efficient Market Theory and the Crisis," *Wall Street Journal*, October 27, Editorial page.

Sloan, R. G. (1996). "Do Stock Prices Fully Reflect Information in Accruals and Cash Flows about Future Earnings?" *The Accounting Review* 71(3), pp. 289–315.

Smith, A. (1967). *The Money Game.* New York, NY: Random House.

Smith, A. (1972). *Supermoney.* New York, NY: Random House.

Solomon, E. (1963). *The Theory of Financial Management.* New York, NY: Columbia University Press.

Stambaugh, R. F. and Yuan, Y. (2017). "Mispricing Factors," *The Review of Financial Studies* 30(4), pp. 1270–1315.

Stattman, D. (1980). "Book Values and Stock Returns," *The Chicago MBA: A Journal of Selected Papers* 4, pp. 25–45.

Summers, L. H. and Summers, V. P. (1989). "When Financial Markets Work Too Well: A Cautious Case for a Securities Tax," *Journal of Financial Services Research* 3(2–3), pp. 261–286.

Taleb, N. (2007). *The Black Swan.* New York, NY: Random House.

Thompson, J. R. and Williams, E. E. (1999). "A Post Keynesian Analysis of the Black-Scholes Option Pricing Model," *The Journal of Post Keynesian Economics* 2, pp. 251–267.

Thompson, J. R., Williams, E. E. and Findlay, M. C. (2003). *Models for Investors in Real World Markets.* New York, NY: John Wiley & Sons.

Tobin, J. (1958). "Liquidity Preference as Behavior Towards Risk," *Review of Economic Studies* 25(2), pp. 65–86.

Tobin, J. (1984). "On the Efficiency of the Financial System," *Lloyds Bank Review* 153, pp. 1–15.

Treynor, J. (1965). "How to Rate Management of Investment Funds," *Harvard Business Review* 43(1), pp. 63–75.

Treynor, J. (1999). "Towards a Theory of Market Value of Risky Assets," in Korajczyk, R. A. (Ed.), *Asset Pricing and Portfolio Performance*, Chapter 2. London, UK: Risk Publications, pp. 15–22. [Originally an unpublished manuscript (1961).]

von Neumann, J. and Morgenstern, O. (1944). *Theory of Games and Economic Behavior*. Princeton, NJ: Princeton University Press.

Weintraub, E. R. (2002). *How Economics Became a Mathematical Science*. Durham: Duke University Press.

Williams, E. E. (2011). "In the Land of the Blind the One-Eyed Are King: How Financial Economics Contributed to the Collapse of 2008–2009," *Journal of Post Keynesian Economics* 34(1), pp. 2–23.

Williams, E. E. and Dobelman, J. A. (2017). *Quantitative Financial Analytics: The Path to Investment Profits*. Hackensack, NJ: World Scientific.

Williams, E. E. and Findlay, M. C. (1974). *Investment Analysis*. Englewood Cliffs, NJ: Prentice-Hall, 1974.

Williams, J. B. (1938). *The Theory of Investment Value*. Amsterdam, the Netherlands: North Holland.

Yen, G. and Lee, C. (2008). "Efficient Market Hypothesis (EMH): Past, Present and Future," *Review of Pacific Basin Financial Markets and Policies* 11(2), pp. 309–329.